Courage

Bob Means

High Tide Publications
Deltaville, Virginia

ISBN: 978-1-962935-15 -9

First Edition 2026

Published by High Tide Publications, Inc.
Deltaville, VA:
https://www.HighTidePublications.com

Cover supplied by the author.

Edited by Carol J. Bova

Printed in the United States of America.

Contents

Forward

On the move again, it was my job as a dozer operator to clear a path for two tanks and two guns to our next destination in Vietnam. We arrived at a village located on the road between Hill 51 and Hill 63 in the Que Son Valley. Several obstacles had to be cleared to get the guns through. After four months in the country, I was a hardcore Marine. I tried to miss the houses in this village, knowing people lived in them.

The tank driver behind me drove through the houses, destroying each one. The ambush at Tam Ky and the tragic loss of innocent lives. Those moments will stay with me forever, burning into my conscience as a warrior. It may have motivated many projects I took on after combat. It was the inspiration for the title of this book.

Courage was a memoir for my descendants to understand who I am. Memories are unreliable and changeable, so I chose to record them. I hope that something in these pages inspires or gives hope to other veterans trying to put the pieces back together after combat.

Bob Means

Memories and Misadventures

My sister and me in front of dad's new car.

Early Memories

The relationship between my father and me was built on fear, not love. When a 2x4 fell from the roof and hit me in the head during one of his construction clean-up jobs, or when I stepped on a nail, he forbade me from crying. Tears were a sign of weakness in his world. When he died years later, I felt nothing—no grief, no sense of loss. I didn't attend his memorial service, and I didn't care.

In my child's mind, rebellion came in the form of crapping in my pants for my revenge. I would shit myself and pretend nothing had happened, carrying the smell with me throughout the entire day.

When he got home from work, the smell hit him right away.

"Did you shit your pants?" he'd demand.

Though we both knew the answer, I would shake my head, lie, and prolong the inevitable.

"Head to the bathroom and wait for me," he would say.

I knew what was coming. He would make me drop my pants, then smear my dirty underwear across my face and make me eat it. The beating with his belt followed, while my sister sat helpless in her rocking chair, tears running down her face as she watched this cycle of cruelty happen again.

Some of my earliest memories come from our small green stucco house in Azusa, California. The unfenced yard contained burn barrels for trash, stark sentinels in the sparse landscape.

My mother would walk me to kindergarten, where I found comfort in coloring rocket ships, dreaming perhaps of escape to distant worlds.

One bright spot during those early years was a wooden airplane my father made for me. I would sit on it and imagine flying through the sky, free from the ground below. One day, I carelessly left it in the neighbor's yard. The next morning, I saw it sticking out of their burn barrel like a broken wing. As I pulled it out of the ashes, I felt anger rush through me for the first time I could remember.

My father worked in construction with Stewart, his brother-in-law, until he earned his contractor's license and decided to go out on his own. Post-war Southern California was booming, filled with people who discovered the region during the war and chose to make it their home. Opportunities were everywhere for a man willing to work.

Eventually, my parents saved enough to buy a house on Studebaker Road, on the outskirts of Long Beach. A bean field stretched out in front, destined to become El Dorado Park in the years to come. Beyond the field, about a mile from our home, lay the San Gabriel Riverbed. A place that would feature prominently in my childhood adventures.

I was fascinated by the team of Mexican workers widening Willow Avenue. Day after day, I watched them form up curb and gutters with practiced precision. They paid me a dollar to carry stakes for the forms they drove into the ground—my first taste of honest work.

My favorite aunt, Barbara, was the only adult who stood up to my father. She would scold him for how he treated me, even though he would always tell her to mind her own business. She also warned us kids never to go near the riverbed, saying that hobos lurked there who might hurt us.

Naturally, we ignored her warnings. During summer days when my parents worked, I'd join the Underhill kids and the Nimnicks for expeditions to the forbidden riverbed. Adventure called, and we answered. It turned out Aunt Barbara's warnings weren't just idle fears.

We were playing under the Willow Street Bridge when he appeared—a weathered hobo moving with predatory purpose. He grabbed the first kid and shook him hard, demanding money. The scared child handed over his quarter and was pushed to the ground. One by one, the hobo took what little money each of us had.

I watched it, too scared to run. When my turn came, I had nothing to offer.

"I don't have any money," I stammered, "but I'll bring a dollar tomorrow."

He threw me down with the others and disappeared as suddenly as he'd come.

Did we learn our lesson? Of course not. We returned to the riverbed again, always on the lookout for hobos. When we saw one, we ran, and I always kept a little money, just in case.

Neighborhood Friends

The sound of the Nimnick children's screams echoed through our neighborhood every evening at five o'clock sharp. Their father believed in preemptive discipline and was convinced his kids must have done something wrong during the day, he'd spank them all as soon as he walked through the door. Hearing their cries drift across the yards, I counted myself lucky not to be born a Nimnick.

Despite the harsh realities some families faced, our neighborhood buzzed with the energy of children at play. My sister and I quickly found our place among the local kids, spending countless hours in games of Army and Cowboys and Indians. We'd gallop around on imaginary horses, and we killed a lot of Indians. When darkness fell, hide-and-seek became our game of choice. I discovered the perfect hiding spot behind the bushes, so perfect that my sister never found me. Eventually, her frustration would boil over, and she'd call out the familiar surrender: "OLE, OLE, OXEN, FREE, FREE, FREE!" Only then would I emerge from my secret sanctuary.

At seven years old, I experienced my first crush on Leslie Brown, whose father was a police officer and who lived just two doors down from me. Every morning, I'd slip out of bed at first light and creep on her front porch, hoping to catch a glimpse of her before the day began. Her mother eventually discovered my vigil and sent me home. Leslie had shown me something that would remain burned in my memory. Leading me behind her house into the bushes, she pulled down her pants. I like that.

***

When I turned nine, our family grew with the arrival of my brother Randy. Aunt Barbara took one look at him and declared he had "the Means' nose." Our family's distinctive features have been passed down to another generation.

The screaming woke me in the middle of the night. Mom's voice cut through the darkness, filled with rage and betrayal. Their marriage was crumbling before my eyes. Dad had opened an office for his construction company and hired a young woman to run it. Mom, consumed by jealousy, accused him of having an affair. She was probably right. Within months, he'd moved out, and she filed for divorce.

The aftermath hit us like a freight train. Mom found work at the Post Office sorting mail, bought a 1953 blue Chevy, and moved us to Circle Garden Apartments near the Long Beach traffic circle. The change devastated my sister Susan, though I can barely recall my own feelings about it. Whatever emotions churned inside me, specific relief was among them.

***

Seventh grade brought me to Stanford Junior High School, while Susan enrolled at Millikan High School. There she met Gary, and they married young, staying together until he drank himself to death.

At Circle Garden Apartments, I met Denny Anderson, who introduced me to "The Dark Side." Under his guidance, we'd meet at 2 AM in the apartment complex garages. He'd break the locks with a sledgehammer, and we'd ransack whatever we found. One garage yielded a treasure trove of fishing gear and a large tackle box. We hauled away everything we could carry, then rode the city bus to Long Beach pier, where we sold the reels and poles to fishermen for a fraction of their value.

But we kept the tackle box filled with pornographic magazines that became my education in things my mother certainly hadn't planned to teach me.

When I turned thirteen, Denny took our adventures to the next level. He convinced me to steal Mom's car keys after she fell asleep, and we'd go joyriding until dawn. I discovered I loved the thrill so much that I stopped waiting for Denny and began taking solo midnight drives.

One morning, everything changed. Returning from a joyride, I found that someone had taken my usual parking space, and I had to park down the block. The next morning, as Mom prepared for work and I ate my Cheerios, she kissed me goodbye and stepped outside.

"WHERE'S MY CAR?!"

I joined her on the porch, feigning innocence.

"Where did you park it, Mom?"

She pointed to the front curb. "Right there!"

"Are you sure?"

"I think I did."

I scanned the street theatrically, then spotted the car where I'd parked it.

"Is that it down there, Mom?"

"It is. How did it get down there?"

"You must have parked it there, Mom."

"I guess I did," she said uncertainly, walking down to retrieve it.

She never questioned it again, but that was my last joyride.

My grades reflected my nocturnal activities. I received C-minuses at best, mostly Ds and Fs. Letters home became routine, as did trips to the dean's office for corporal punishment. I was carousing at night and binge drinking on weekends. The police picked me up multiple times, forcing Mom to collect me from the station.

Finally, she'd had enough. "You're going to live with your father."

Life with Dad and Mary

Dad was rebuilding his life after bankruptcy and was now married to Mary, my stepmother. They lived in a cramped apartment in San Clemente with Mary's daughter and their baby, Janis. I was clearly an unwelcome addition to their already tight quarters.

Dad was constructing apartment buildings for Dr. Meyer, and when I wasn't in school, I helped with the construction. He drove me hard, and his boot found my backside whenever I failed to meet his exacting standards.

Capo High School was divided between two distinct groups: the Mexicans and the surfers. I gravitated toward the surfers, though Dad considered them "the most worthless people on the planet." Still, he'd let me surf after completing my chores, knowing how much I loved it and using that passion as leverage to extract hard work from me.

My grades improved marginally. I saved every penny to buy a new Yordy surfboard with a wood tail block, and we moved into one of Dad's newly constructed apartments.

That's when President Kennedy was assassinated. Dad was devastated because he and JFK had both served on PT boats during the war, creating a bond that transcended politics.

Dad's next project involved building apartments for an investment group in Carlsbad. One of the partners was Sandy Koufax, the legendary pitcher for the Dodgers. Dad and Sandy played golf together several times, and once he let me drive their golf cart.

Reaching for an Oreo cookie on the dashboard, I somehow managed to run straight into Sandy Koufax, knocking him to the ground. Dad's fury was legendary. I never touched a golf cart again.

***

We relocated to Carlsbad, where I transferred to Carlsbad High School. I quickly infiltrated the local surfing crowd and landed a job managing the varsity football team. After one game, several surfer friends and I attended a party and got spectacularly drunk.

I could barely stand when I arrived home. Stopping to urinate before heading upstairs, I forgot to zip up afterward. Hoping Dad and Mary had gone to bed, I crept through the front door, only to find them watching television, waiting for me.

I attempted a brief goodnight, but Mary's sharp eyes caught my wardrobe malfunction.

"WHAT IS YOUR DICK DOING OUT OF YOUR PANTS?!" Dad bellowed.

Our already strained relationship reached its breaking point. When I said I wanted to go back to Mom's, Dad reached into his pocket, pulled out a five-dollar bill, and told me to pack my things. He drove me to the bus station without saying another word.

That night, I found myself back in Long Beach.

Mom had her own complications; she'd married Bill Marks, a colorful character who'd served in the Merchant Marines. At the war's outbreak, he'd worked as a machinist on a ship off Egypt's coast. Captured by Germans in Alexandria, Egypt, he spent the war's remainder in a prison camp in Krakow, proudly displaying his tattooed prison number.

Mom adored Bill despite his problems. In drunken stupors, he created intricately detailed sailing ships and somehow maneuvered them into bottles. From a pine block, he carved a British man-of-war complete with tiny cannons. He was undeniably an artist, a likable drunk, but a drunk, nonetheless.

His masterpiece was a Monterey boat hull he discovered sunk in fifteen feet of water. Using inner tubes and an air hose, while completely intoxicated, he raised the hull and restored it. He moved it to 7th Street Landing in Long Beach, transforming it into a "Gypsy Boat," a true classic. Bill significantly influenced my life, though I never did master his secret burrito recipe.

Life at 7th Street Landing

Though I enrolled at Poly High School, I spent most of my time at 7th Street Landing, a place with its own unique ecosystem. The Barge Bar greeted visitors at the entrance, where drunken women performed nightly strip shows. At the dock's far end sat a houseboat where a father auctioned his daughters to the highest bidders while his wife worked.

One family living on their boat had two daughters. I had strong feelings for Barbara, unaware that Poly High's star running back shared my affection. While we were making out on Bill's boat's foredeck, the football player appeared and beat me senseless.

Humiliated and furious, I wanted revenge. The problem was obvious; I stood 5'2" and weighed 118 pounds. The next day, I convinced Mom to drive me to the Marine Corps recruiting office. I wanted to join the Marines, learn to fight, and return to settle the score.

Mom was surprisingly happy to oblige.

The Marines

Graduation - Marine Boot Camp - 1965

Marine Boot Camp

If you never experienced Marine Corps boot camp in the mid-sixties, you couldn't imagine in your wildest dreams that a place like this existed on the planet.

In what should have been the summer between my junior and senior years, I entered the gates of MCRD San Diego on July 5th, 1965. I was seventeen years and two months old.

On a sunny, pleasant morning, a group of recruits gathered outside the recruiter's office in downtown Long Beach. A chartered bus was parked on the street. Friends and family came to bid us farewell. In his dress blue uniform, the recruiter moved through the crowd, speaking with families, answering questions, and engaging in small talk. It was peaceful.

Recruits were told to board the bus, sit down, and bring only the clothes on their backs. Everything we needed would be supplied upon our arrival. I sat next to Icorn, who wore black Frisco jeans, a dirty white T-shirt, and a wide leather belt strapped around his waist under his armpits. We didn't know each other, but we soon would.

As the bus pulled away, I watched Mom crying through the window.

The trip to San Diego was quiet. We each sat silently, lost in our own thoughts. There was a war happening in Vietnam, and we were headed straight for it. The recruiter sat in the front seat next to the driver.

When the bus reached the middle of the parade grounds, our recruiter wished us good luck. We never saw him again.

Through the windows, we saw five sharply dressed Marines in khaki uniforms with spit-shined shoes, all wearing Smokey Bear hats. At parade rest, they stood in a perfect line, looking straight ahead with blank expressions. They were non-commissioned officers (NCOs) with combat ribbons on their chests.

One tall Marine Gunnery Sergeant stood at the front, wearing blue trousers, a khaki shirt, and many ribbons. This 6'8" man with a strong physique embodied the ideal Marine. He jumped on the bus, marking the start.

In no uncertain terms, using the most commanding voice, he told us that no one was to speak unless spoken to. Our eyes were to stay directly ahead. When ordered to get off the bus, we were to move to the yellow footprints painted on the concrete, stand on those footprints facing the bus with our eyes forward, remain silent, and keep our hands by our sides.

As we exited the bus, the other drill instructors greeted us while charging around like Tasmanian Devils. They were in our faces, two of them on each side of our heads, screaming in our ears. "GET YOUR FEET ON THOSE YELLOW FOOTPRINTS YOU GOD DAMN MAGGOT! WHAT THE FUCK ARE YOU LOOKING AT, YOU FAGGOT? ARE YOU IN LOVE WITH ME? YOU WANT TO FUCK ME? KEEP YOUR EYEBALLS STRAIGHT AHEAD, YOU LITTLE TURD!"

Shitbird, maggot, and puke were the favorites. Icorn took the worst of it. He shouldn't have gotten off that bus with his belt cinched up under his armpits.

The Drill Instructors were finally satisfied as we stood on our yellow footprints. The Gunnery Sergeant stood in front and told us to obey every order given. For example, he ordered the Corporal standing beside him to strike him in the face. The Corporal struck him with a mighty blow. At that point, we had no doubt what we'd gotten ourselves into.

We learned a new language. The first thing out of our mouths was to be "SIR!" as in "SIR! YES SIR!" or "SIR! NO SIR!" The request for permission to speak was "SIR! PRIVATE MEANS REQUESTS PERMISSION TO SPEAK TO THE DRILL INSTRUCTOR, SIR!" in the loudest voice one could produce.

The first stop was at the barber shop. We walked in single file, eyes straight ahead, and no one spoke. They shaved our heads. We marched to the showers, turned in our civilian clothes, and were issued white skivvies.

After the shower, we put on the skivvies, moved to another line, and received socks, tennis shoes, green utility trousers, a yellow sweatshirt, and a green utility cover.

The next stop was the chow hall. The first Marine Corps meal consisted of meat, potatoes, gravy, and vegetables, served on a metal tray. We were instructed where to sit at long tables with benches on each side and told how to dispose of our metal trays and silverware when finished. No talking or looking around was allowed. We were given five minutes to eat before being back outside in formation.

Our "street" had Quonset huts facing each other. Each of us was assigned to a hut. Inside were metal bunk beds with springs and a three-inch mattress, with wooden footlockers underneath to keep our gear. We were instructed to make a proper rack (bed) with a fart sack and hospital corners tucked tight and squared away. Thus, our training began. If the Drill Instructor (DI) couldn't bounce a quarter off the tight blanket, he tore it apart. After fifty pushups, you started over.

Clyde McDonald and I were bunkmates through boot camp and the Infantry Training Regiment. I slept on the top rack; he was on the bottom. He was killed on his third day in Vietnam after stepping on a landmine.

It was midnight before we were settled in our new home, and then it was lights out.

The next morning, we met our drill instructors, who were tasked with training us to be Marines: Staff Sergeant Loo, Sergeant Prather, and Corporal Eastman. They offered nothing to like about them. They had a job to do. They were professionals.

At 0400, lights came on, a metal trash can flew across the Quonset hut, bouncing off metal racks, and the DI screamed, "GET OUT OF THOSE FUCKING RACKS, YOU MAGGOTS!" Any hesitation resulted in the DI rushing to the bunk and turning it over onto the deck, the recruit still in it. One could get hurt, but it taught us a valuable lesson.

Training began with learning right from left and close-order drill. We were taught which foot to start with, how to stay in step, and how to move from column right to column left to the rear march. If you failed to get it right, you performed many squat thrusts and push-ups. The order of the day included PT and a two-mile run before first light, morning chow, more PT, and more close-order drills. Quonset huts must always be spotless, and racks must be tight.

Classes covered every aspect of the Marine Corps. We had medical and dental checkups, lots of shots, and cavity fillings. Weapons were issued, and we were taught to clean, carry, and run with them during two-mile runs in formation. On bad days, the two-mile run would turn into a five-mile run, with our gear on in the hot sun. If someone fell out, he was carried by everybody else. Icorn fell out, and two recruits had to carry him.

We ran through obstacles, not around them. We survived bayonet training with puggle sticks, a stick with two pads on either side. We attacked each other until the DI said one of us was killed. The grueling obstacle course was run in any weather and had to be finished within a prescribed time. Weakness wasn't tolerated, with no mercy for failure. We were taught to kill with our bare hands.

The two smallest members of our platoon were designated House Mouse. I was 5'2", 118 pounds, and Gary Lopez was slightly bigger. We were chosen. Our job was to clean and tidy up the drill instructors' hut and polish their shoes. We dispensed Band-Aids and medicine for the sick during morning formation and roll call.

In Vietnam, Lopez received a medal for single-handedly holding off a frontal attack by the North Vietnamese Army up a hill during Operation Hastings.

To enter the drill instructors' hut, we pounded three times on a small wooden block next to the hatch (door) with our fists as hard as we could. Quonset huts were made of metal. One needed to use enough force so that the sound reverberated throughout the hut. Then we'd shout at the top of our lungs, "SIR, PRIVATE MEANS REQUESTS PERMISSION TO ENTER THE DRILL INSTRUCTOR'S HUT, SIR!" If not loud enough, the request was ignored, forcing us to repeat the whole procedure, sometimes multiple times.

Midway through boot camp, we were packed up and loaded into cattle cars for the rifle range at Camp Edson, where we were instructed on how to fire the M-14, a gas-operated, magazine-fed rifle with 20 rounds of 7.62 mm ammunition. We were shown the characteristics of this fine weapon, how to sight it, and how to snap in from the prone, sitting, and standing positions at 100, 300, and 500 yards.

In the butts, they raised and lowered the targets, marking where the round hit. Missing the target got you a red flag, called Maggie's Drawers, waved across the target. Competition was intense among the other platoons. It was important for our platoon to score high. If not, we paid the price by suiting up in our gear, including rifles, and duck-walking while holding our rifles high, sending the message that our scores had to improve. Our platoon came in last.

Staff Sergeant Loo made Icorn a house mouse because he screwed up so much. He charged Lopez and me with squaring him away. We did our best. It wasn't easy because he was so dumb.

Going out to the range, I told Icorn to enter the drill instructors' hut and ensure everything was squared away. I should have checked, but I was tied up with other assigned duties. Returning, I heard Staff Sergeant Loo yell out, "HEAD HOUSE MOUSE TO THE DRILL INSTRUCTOR'S HUT!"

I was the head house mouse. I removed my shooting jacket and, in my white T-shirt, dropped everything and ran to the duty hut. Staff Sergeant Loo struck his open palm with a coat hanger that Icorn had left on the drill instructor's rack. Staff Sergeant Loo asked me if I knew where he had found the coat hanger.

"NO SIR!"

He began striking me across the neck with the coat hanger. He asked me if the end of his rack was the correct position for the coat hanger.

"NO SIR!"

Striking harder, he broke my skin. I began to bleed. The blood on my T-shirt made me technically out of uniform.

"BLOOD IS ON YOUR T-SHIRT, YOU MAGGOT! YOU ARE OUT OF UNIFORM. YOU TURD. GET YOUR ASS DOWN AND GIVE ME A HUNDRED PUSHUPS, PUKE!"

"AYE, AYE, SIR!"

I took the punishment for Icorn because I was the head house mouse. It was my responsibility.

Completing my hundred push-ups, Sergeant Prather ordered Lopez and me to take Icorn into the broom closet and beat the shit out of him, which I was more than happy to do.

Because Icorn wasn't taking showers, we were punished with 200 squat thrusts while Icorn stood in front, counting. A group dragged Icorn into the head, giving him a military shower with heavy scrub brushes.

On Visitor's Day, our families and girlfriends came to see how we were getting on. Refreshments were served at a small recreation center. Dad and Mary came and gave me my driver's license. He wouldn't let me have it while I lived with him.

David Brown's girlfriend came. Afterward, she stopped on Highway 101 just off the base. David waited until dark, then snuck out to meet his girlfriend. The next morning at roll call, he was gone. He had gone AWOL, but it wasn't the last time we saw David.

The makeup of a platoon's uniforms illustrated its stage of training. New arrivals had green utility trousers, yellow T-shirts, tennis shoes, and a green cover. After a week of training, we received a green utility blouse buttoned at the top and black boots. Trouser legs hanging down over the top of the boot are called "Unbloused."

At the rifle range, we bloused our boots, tucking our trouser legs under themselves to the top of the boot, and unbuttoned the top button of our shirts. Returning from the rifle range, we were fitted for dress uniforms in preparation for the close-order drill competition. We were judged on our marching abilities as we passed in review before generals and dignitaries.

In the final two weeks, we starched our covers. We looked and felt like real Marines. But there was still a lot to go through. My worst day at boot camp happened at this time.

Afternoon chow, while marching back to our squad bay, my stomach started to rumble. Back in our area, Staff Sergeant Loo barked out, "Okay, you maggots, the smoking lamp is lit."

"SIR, SMOKING LAMP IS LIT, AYE, AYE SIR."

Man, I had to shit.

It was summer, and our faces were tanned except for the tops of our heads, which were protected by our covers. Our foreheads were as white as a sheet. Staff Sergeant Loo didn't like that. He was a Guamanian with a dark complexion and felt we should look like him.

"All right, you shitbirds, take off those covers. Get some sun on those heads so you look like me."

"SIR, AYE, AYE, SIR."

Taking off our covers, we slid the bill under our belts and trousers in the small of our backs.

I yelled, "SIR, PRIVATE MEANS REQUESTS PERMISSION TO SPEAK TO THE DRILL INSTRUCTOR, SIR."

"SPEAK, YOU LITTLE TURD."

"SIR, PRIVATE MEANS REQUESTS PERMISSION TO GO TO THE HEAD, SIR."

"HURRY UP, YOU SHITBIRD, AND GET BACK HERE BEFORE THE SMOKING LAMP IS OUT!"

"SIR, AYE, AYE, SIR."

I had to go so badly that I didn't know if I would make it. I ran onto the head, undoing my trousers as I went, skidding to the toilet just in time to let it rip. Jesus, that felt good. Wiping my ass, I stood to flush.

Looking into the commode, I couldn't believe what I saw. I said out loud, "Who's the asshole that put his cover in the toilet?"

Then it hit me.

"OH GOD! OH, GOD! PLEASE GOD!"

After retrieving my cover, I cleaned it, hearing, "OK, MAGGOTS, THE SMOKING LAMP IS OUT."

Running to formation as fast as I could, I stuffed my dripping wet cover into the back of my belt, just in time for the "AYE, AYE SIR."

We stood in the hot sun with freshly starched covers stuffed in our belts, except mine. The dreaded moment came:

"GET YOUR COVERS BACK ON YOUR HEAD, MAGGOTS!"

"SIR, AYE, AYE, SIR!"

The next sound we heard was, "MEANS! WHAT IN THE FUCK DID YOU DO TO YOUR COVER?"

Graduation

Our platoon couldn't shoot worth a damn, but we knew how to do close order drill, which we won wearing our newly tailored dress uniforms. It was a proud moment for our platoon, with the generals and dignitaries watching. And it was the first time we saw Staff Sergeant Loo smile.

Graduation was a week away. The DIs began to let down, becoming halfway human. We turned in our gear and learned how to fold our new uniforms, pack them in a sea bag, and get them pressed and cleaned for the big event. We had rehearsal after rehearsal. It was almost over.

Graduation day was a big event on the main parade ground. Friends and family filled the bleachers. Generals and officers lined up in front, standing at attention as the color guard passed in review.

The Marine Band played the Marine Corps Hymn as we marched around the parade ground, coming to a halt in front of the bleachers: right face, parade rest. A general gave a speech congratulating us on a job well done. We were finished.

After the festivities, we packed up for the final time. The next day, we'd be bused to Camp Pendleton for the Infantry Training Regiment, where we'd learn to fight and fire every weapon the Marine Corps had.

We'd be called Marines.

David Brown arrived to retrieve his gear, handcuffed, with two armed guards on either side of him. He was off to the brig.

Infantry Training Regiment

Training was intense: throwing hand grenades, firing flame throwers, M-240 and M-60 machine guns, breaking them down, and cleaning them. We endured twenty-mile forced marches at night with full gear, learning infantry tactics, night maneuvers, crawling under barbed wire on our backs with live fire thirty inches over our heads, and explosives going off around us. We charged up mountains, firing blanks and attacking machine gun emplacements. They fired back with blanks. I was soaked in sweat.

Walking down trails, we fired live ammo at pop-up targets and used night scopes. We were taught how to identify booby traps.

On our first liberty, wearing my uniform, I went home to see my mom and hang out with friends. I saw Paul, who had beaten me up for making out with Barbara on Bill's boat. We shook hands and then got drunk. I forgot all about why I joined the Marines in the first place. Now I am stuck with four years in the Marines.

A Real Marine, 1st FSR

Being a Marine was a high calling. One that would send us off to slaughter.

When I reported to the staging battalion to be shipped overseas, I arrived at night during a torrential rainstorm. The taxi dropped me off in my dress uniform, a whole sea bag of gear weighing me down. I didn't know where to go. Confused and overwhelmed, I sat down on my sea bag and cried, getting soaked to the bone. A Marine ran past, seeking shelter from the rain, but he took pity on me and pointed out where to check in.

The clerk sent me to the barracks to find a rack. Icorn, Lopez, and McDonald were already there with the rest of my buddies. We were all 0311 infantry riflemen, bound for war.

It took several days to complete the paperwork for our journey across the Pacific to Okinawa, where we would receive jungle training as replacements for Marines returning home or those killed in combat.

In the morning, when we were scheduled to leave, we stood in formation as cattle car buses pulled up to transport us to El Toro Marine Air Base. I was tenth in line, directly behind McDonald. A Corporal emerged from the office, calling my name. He ordered me to report to the office and wait.

Having no idea what was happening, I watched helplessly as the other Marines I'd trained with— including Icorn, Lopez, and McDonald-boarded the bus and drove away.

After what felt like an eternity, a clerk approached the counter and asked me to step forward. Congress had recently passed a law: no more seventeen-year-olds could be sent to war. I had to wait until I turned eighteen.

They changed my Military Occupational Specialty (MOS) from infantry to 1345—Heavy Equipment Operator. I was now a Marine engineer reporting to the 1st Force Service Regiment, Engineer Section.

I was devastated not to be able to go with my buddies to Okinawa and the Northern Training Area.

1st FSR: Learning the Trade

The 1st FSR was a backwater engineer maintenance unit that repaired and maintained Marine machinery. It wasn't the Marine Corps I was used to, or the one I'd dreamed of joining.

When I checked in, the First Sergeant assigned me a bunk. After 1600 hours, other Marines filtered back into the barracks, and I met those I'd be working alongside. John Dom from Ohio was a welder, married, and living off base. Vail Thompson from Klamath Falls, Oregon, was in the same predicament as I: he was seventeen. Our Commanding Officer was a mustang 2nd Lieutenant determined to make a name for himself, and he wasn't easily pleased.

My first assignment as a 1345 heavy equipment operator was to learn to operate and maintain a diverse array of equipment, including bulldozers, cranes, road graders, forklifts, generators of various shapes and sizes, as well as jeeps and two-and-a-half-ton trucks. I had to master their operation and maintenance schedules to obtain my license. During my first month, I spent most of my time greasing fittings with a grease gun, as there wasn't much else to do.

The company's Gunnery Sergeant was Gunny Buck, a burly old-timer who knew his equipment inside and out. He established a heavy equipment operating school so that guys like Vail and me could become proficient in our trade.

We started with bulldozers, heading into the hills to cut away hillsides and carve out rough roads. The cranes were more enjoyable, lifting massive generators and placing them precisely on truck beds.

Road graders proved trickier and far more temperamental, but I gradually developed a feel for the work.

Gunny Buck designed realistic field operations under simulated combat conditions. When Reserve units came to train, we played the enemy force.

After six months of the same routine, day after day, we knew our equipment like the back of our hands. I developed itchy feet and wanted to move on. My eighteenth birthday was approaching, and I told Gunny Buck I wanted to go to Vietnam. He promised to see what he could do.

Twenty-Nine Palms: 5th 155 Guns

Just as I was getting restless, the Marine Corps activated the 5th Division to prosecute the war in Vietnam more effectively.

I transferred to Twenty-Nine Palms Marine Base to join the 5th 155 Gun Battery (Self-Propelled). I assumed I'd eventually be transferred to the 1st or 3rd Engineers, who were already operating in Vietnam.

I knew nothing about self-propelled artillery. John Dom, the welder from my previous unit, received orders for 5th Guns simultaneously. We were the tenth and eleventh Marines to report to this newly formed unit; they hadn't yet received their guns. We were assigned to the maintenance section.

The desert heat was brutal. There wasn't much beyond the Marine base itself. The unit gradually took shape as more personnel arrived. Two TD-15 dozers arrived, and I was assigned to one of them. The same model I'd trained on at 1st FSR.

I began with the familiar routine: greasing the fittings and changing the oil in the idlers. The other operator was named Stevens. We took our dozers into the desert and dug holes—our job was to ensure the guns could get into position, dig gun emplacements and ammunition pits, and handle whatever else bulldozers needed to do.

The guns finally arrived, looking like massive tanks with long barrels protruding from enclosed turrets at the rear.

A full roster of Marine artillerymen conducted desert firing operations lasting up to a week. Stevens and I would dig the gun and ammunition pits at designated locations. The guns would move in, set up, fire several rounds, then relocate and repeat the process.

After field training exercises, we'd return to our maintenance area, unpack everything, and perform equipment maintenance. On weekends, we played brutal tackle football games, beating ourselves up badly in the process.

Our unit participated in a major war game involving infantry, tanks, and jet aircraft attacking an imaginary enemy. The infantry sent fire missions around the clock. I'm pretty sure we won.

Next Stop: Vietnam

Vietnam - 1967

Shipping Out

When orders came to be deployed overseas, we packed our equipment in massive wooden shipping crates bearing special military identification markings. These were loaded onto military flatbed trucks forming a lengthy convoy bound for San Diego Naval Base, where the *USS Ogden* awaited us.

The O gden w as N avy-designated a s a n L PD (Landing P ad D ock). Newly commissioned, it was designed specifically for amphibious landings. A cavernous cargo area occupied the rear section, with a helicopter landing pad covering the ship's back half. The stern featured a massive gate that could open and submerge to launch Amtracs (Amphibious Tractors) and smaller landing craft.

On November 22, 1966, we cast off into the western Pacific with everything aboard: guns, dozers, trucks, jeeps, and all the equipment needed for a combat unit. Our destination remained officially unknown, though we had a pretty good idea where we were headed.

Despite calm seas, half our Marines got seasick.

Pearl Harbor and Okinawa

Brand-New Eimco 103-Mark M-64 Dozer

We stopped at Pearl Harbor, where most of the unit got three days of liberty. After being kicked out of several bars for being only eighteen, I rented a surfboard and went surfing instead. I tried teaching a few of our guys how to surf, but they didn't fare too well.

Eight days later, off the coast of Okinawa, Japan, we were stationed at Camp Hansen, where there was little to occupy our time. The island was too small for our guns' firing range.

Stevens and I received two brand-new Eimco 103-mark M-64 bulldozers. This model positioned the operator up front, giving them a clear view over the blade. We spent our time mastering maintenance procedures and operating techniques. They were impressive machines, powered by a 361 Jimmy Diesel engine capable of reaching eight miles per hour.

Outside Camp Hansen lay Kin Village, where half the establishments were bars and brothels staffed with Japanese prostitutes charging three dollars. As an eighteen-year-old male, I felt like a kid in a candy store. We ran in formation to stay in shape, but we had other activities in mind for our off-duty hours.

Okinawan bars lacked modern plumbing. To relieve yourself, you used the binjo ditches out back. Local farmers would collect the waste to fertilize their rice fields.

One night, John Dom, Baron Clark, and I were walking back to base after heavy drinking when we discovered someone passed out in a binjo ditch. When we pulled him out, we recognized our commanding officer, Major Coyal. Everyone knew about his drinking problem.

We hired a taxi and loaded him in. He reeked, and we worried about trouble if the MPs stopped us at the gate. We showed our liberty cards to the guards, who waved us through. We directed the cabbie to the officers' quarters, dragged the unconscious major to the locked front door, propped him against the wall, and retreated to our barracks. He never stirred, and we never said a word to anyone. Major Coyal was relieved shortly afterward, replaced by Major Black.

Frequenting bars and brothels every night devastated our paychecks. I decided to buy swim fins, a mask, and a snorkel at the base PX. Walking to the water's edge, I dove into crystal-clear, warm water teeming with coral and beautiful tropical fish. Soon, several of our guys joined me. Unfortunately, an Okinawan discovered our clothes on the beach and stole our money, which infuriated us.

Mount Fuji

Orders arrived to pack up for Mount Fuji, Japan. The Marines maintained a base at the volcano's foot where we could finally fire our guns. We loaded onto ancient flat-bottom Landing Ship Tanks (LSTs). Ours was LST-1166, a World War II leftover.

When we approached Numazu Beach, Japanese protesters had organized a demonstration demanding that the Marine base at Mount Fuji be shut down. We were instructed to behave in a manner that would not upset the locals.

Before beaching, we went below decks to prepare our vehicles for unloading. My dozer was first off, the ramp. As the ship struck the beach, the bow doors opened, and the ramp lowered. I was terrified, expecting to face a thousand screaming Japanese protesters. Instead, the "mob" consisted of four elderly Japanese men holding signs reading "Yankee Go Home." I rolled down the ramp, almost disappointed.

That night on the beach, before proceeding to Mount Fuji, a larger crowd gathered and began chanting, "YANKEE GO HOME!" Every time they did, we cheered back—not exactly our best behavior.

Mount Fuji was breathtaking. On clear mornings, I gazed up at the perfectly shaped cone with its snow-covered peak. Oil-burning stoves took the chill off cold nights in our tents, which were draped over wooden frames. We ate C-rations exclusively.

Gatimba was a charming little town just outside the base. Further down the road lay Takigahara, where small bars lined the main street. Bar girls would sit with you while you drank beer, and the brothels were tucked away on back roads—much fancier than Okinawa's establishments, but considerably more expensive.

An orphanage was located on the far side of the mountain in the Five Lakes area. Marines had helped support it since the end of World War II. When we visited, we played with the children, and each of us gave the matron five dollars upon our departure.

Several of us bought train tickets to Tokyo, staying in a fancy hotel and taking tour buses to see the sights. Everything appeared three-quarters the size of American equivalents. In restaurants, we ordered by pointing to wax replicas of meals. Finding prostitutes proved difficult; they charged sixteen dollars, more than we could afford. Every night, we got thoroughly drunk in Ginga, Tokyo's entertainment district.

The following week, after firing and calibrating our guns, we loaded our gear and returned to the beach and the LST for the trip back to Okinawa.

Destination: Vietnam

On The Way To Vietnam

In Okinawa, we unpacked just long enough to be issued jungle utilities and jungle boots, then were ordered to repack everything. Being denied liberty was disappointing, so we got drunk at the enlisted men's club, where girls danced for a dime.

After loading our gear onto trucks, we traveled to Naha harbor, where the LSD Catamount waited. It took several days to get everything aboard before the Catamount weighed anchor.

Our next stop: the Republic of South Vietnam.

Before departing, I was promoted to Lance Corporal. I was moving up in the world.

Hill 51, Vietnam

1st Battalion, 5th Marines On Hill 51

We landed at the bridge ramp in Da Nang sometime in 1967, unloading guns, vehicles, and equipment via Landing Craft Utilities (LCUs) and camping on the beach for three nights. We didn't realize that no one in the division knew we were coming. Years later, I discovered that fact, and I guess that's why they didn't know what to do with us when we arrived.

Major Black, our Battery CO, announced, "All right, they're splitting us up. Listen up for your platoon assignments."

He called up three captains to be COs of different platoons: HQ Platoon, 1st Platoon, and 2nd Platoon. Each platoon received two 155mm self-propelled guns. It was like being chosen for a neighborhood flag football game, with each captain calling out the names of gun crews, FDC personnel, drivers, and dozer operators. As dozer operators, McCoy went to HQ Platoon, Stevens to 1st Platoon, and I was assigned to 2nd Platoon.

Captain Steen was our Platoon CO. Nobody knew him because he'd been with another unit. Lieutenant Wasson was our XO (Executive Officer). Until then, I didn't know either of them.

We huddled around our prospective officers, who provided us with lists of equipment and supplies to gather from the general store. Our equipment was organized in neat piles and loaded onto an LCU bound for Que Son Valley to join the 1/5 (1st Battalion, 5th Marines) on Hill 51. The HQ Battery was headed to a ROK (Republic of Korea) Marine compound below Chu Lai. The 1st Platoon was going to Dong Ha, just below the DMZ.

With everything loaded, the LCU backed out late in the afternoon, heading for the open sea through Da Nang Harbor. Monkey Mountain stood on our right as we headed south through the waters around Monkey Point. Darkness set in.

We tried to sleep, but I was excited and kept visiting the galley for more coffee. My buddy pointed toward land, where a Puff (DC-3 armed with miniguns) was firing a few miles inland. We could see the solid line of red tracers and hear the roar of miniguns sounding like an engine running. We were now in Vietnam, finally joining the real war. It hit home that men were fighting and dying just beyond our vision as we watched from offshore.

The next day, we reached Chu Lai, unloaded, and traveled a short distance to a group of buildings. The first smell was of burning latrines, a smell we became accustomed to.

After receiving ammunition, we pitched in, loading the guns with 155mm rounds and powder canisters. Staff Sergeant Snowman, the acting Gunny, informed me that the 9th Engineers were transporting my dozer to Hill 63, and someone from a 105mm outfit would pick me up.

Early the next day, the guns took off with the 1st Tanks. Alone with my dozer and my gear stacked on top, I felt sad as the guns pulled out. Our gun platoon hadn't gelled yet, but I still wanted to be with my unit.

A flatbed showed up, and I loaded my dozer onto it. Behind them, a few Marines in a small jeep called a Mighty Mite came roaring in. They got out and introduced themselves—they'd come to take me out to Hill 63.

Right off the bat, I noticed how "unsquared away" they were. Their trousers weren't bloused. Their jungle boots hadn't seen polish in months, and the toes were white with wear. They were bush Marines! But they were both lance corporals, like me. I felt a sting of jealousy and wished my boots looked as good as theirs.

They were anxious to take off soon and return to Hill 63 before dark, but first, they wanted chow. We headed for the chow hall as the engineers took off with my dozer. Thankfully, breakfast was still being served.

We filled our trays and found a table as they clued me in on in-country life in the bush. One guy already had a Purple Heart from a shrapnel wound the night they got mortared. They got a kick out of sharing their war stories with this new guy.

I just kept responding with stuff like, "Really, man?" "Geez!" and "No kidding."

The ride on Highway 1 to Hill 63 wasn't bad, but it was secure, with 9th Engineers keeping the road open. After Hill 63, however, the road to Hill 51 in Que Son Valley could be challenging, real Indian country.

We picked up another guy in the Mighty Mite, making four of us. The two of us in the back were crowded with our rifles and 782 gear. As we sped through Chu Lai compound past the airstrip, we saw jets take off. Choppers were overhead with the familiar "wop, wop" of their rotor blades. That sound became very familiar.

Leaving the main gate, turning right onto Highway 1, the village streets were crowded with Vietnamese people. Women carried two baskets suspended from a pole resting on their shoulders. Everything was carried in those baskets, from pigs to firewood. Bars and brothels were everywhere. The MPs were already patrolling the streets, and lots of Army guys were cruising the bars and brothels.

Once through Chu Lai, we were on the open road. The driver was going so fast that it was hard to take in the countryside, which was lush and beautiful, with rice paddies, women, and water buffalo working the fields. We passed Cham and Buddhist temples, dark green hills, and quaint villages.

"Man, I'm really here. Hard to believe!" I thought to myself. "Hot—it's getting hot!"

A detour went off the main road. The driver didn't see it coming and took the turn way too fast. We spun out, dust so thick I couldn't see. His buddy told him he'd better slow down, but before long, he was speeding up again.

Coming upon a Marine jeep with only the driver, we slowed down. In the jeep was Gunny Buck from 1st FSR.

Recognizing each other, he said, "Means, are you still a lance corporal?"

He shook his head and drove off.

We arrived at Hill 63, where we met up with the guns and tanks. Gun crews were excited because they'd received small arms fire twice. One tank driver took a round in his helmet that spun around the inside but never penetrated the skin.

My dozer was there. I unloaded it from the flatbed. Captain Steen came over asking if I'd carry something for him.

"Aye, aye, sir."

His future father-in-law, a chief warrant officer with the Marine Air Wing at Da Nang, had given Steen a spring rack with a mattress. He wanted to load it on top of my dozer with the other cargo. I lashed it down with communication wire, the best I could.

My dozer had a big Jimmy Diesel behind the driver's seat with two exhaust pipes coming through the top on either side. I packed as much stuff as I could between those pipes, including Captain Steen's rack. We left for Hill 51 at first light with a contingent of 2nd Battalion 5th Marines and a couple of tanks.

The trip to Hill 51 was uneventful, except for a river crossing that required me to fill in. The sides were quite steep, and Captain Steen's rack shifted while I was working. His mattress caught fire when it met my exhaust pipes. I cut the communication wire as fast as possible, throwing everything off.

His rack and mattress were ruined. My sea bag never made it back on, so I had no change of clothes for quite some time. The underwear wasn't a problem; we never wore any because it was too hot. The problem was the lack of socks and trousers.

Getting to Hill 51 late in the afternoon, I felt truly in-country. Hill 51 sat in the Que Son Valley, with mountain ridges on either side. A small village to the right of the compound looked up the valley. The village had formed around the main gate, where a road passed by. The Ly-Ly River meandered down the valley on the opposite side of the compound, with rice paddies lining each side of the river. Green, green, it was so green.

The road wasn't more than a wide dirt path. Years later, in 1988, when I returned to visit, the road was paved and lined with gum trees forty feet high. Our Vietnamese guides told us the road was named American Road because Army Engineers had built it up and paved it.

The CP tent was located to the right of the compound entrance, where Colonel Hilgartner and Lieutenant Colonel Meachum were stationed. A platoon of 1st Tanks was right next to their tent. To the left was a large, open area that was part of a Vietnamese graveyard, with fallow rice paddies below. In the middle were two large clumps of granite boulders. The 105mm and 155mm towed units and ammo pit were positioned in the saddle between the boulders.

Infantry companies were dispersed around the compound, with a small LZ between the tanks and 105mm gun pits. Only one tree stood inside the whole area. The compound was surrounded by rows and rows of barbed wire and outposts (OPs) thirty yards apart.

Ten grunts were riding on my dozer when we arrived—they were suffering from heat prostration. Man, was it hot! I mean, hot!

I was glad to get there finally, but the barbed wire surrounding the entry gave only a false sense of security. Through the two clumps of boulders, past the 105mm pits, there was a grassy, sloping hillside. That was our home for the next few months.

Settling in, we took stock of our gear and surroundings. It was getting dark. At the chow tent, they prepared a meal for us. We laid our ponchos on the open ground and fell asleep. It felt good to be somewhere.

The next day was a beehive of activity. I set to work with my dozer, scraping flat areas to pitch the tents. Then I dug out the side of the hill for the FDC bunker, gun pits, and ammo pits. Guns were backed into the pits and calibrated for aiming stakes. Choppers flew in 155mm ammo and powder canisters, and we stacked them neatly in the ammo pits. Each round weighed 98 to 110 pounds.

There were hundreds of sandbags. They surrounded each tent, as well as ammo pits, gun pits, the FDC bunker, and even the water trailer (also known as the "water buffalo"), all of which were protected by sandbags. If that wasn't enough, we filled sandbags for the sake of filling sandbags.

Man! Was it hot!

Fire missions began on the first night, every three hours. These were H&I (Harassing and Interdiction) missions. We weren't shooting at anything specific; we were aiming at probable approach areas, never knowing the actual target. We fired two rounds, secured the gun, and went back to bed. Two hours later, the command "FIRE MISSION!" came from the FDC (Fire Direction Control) bunker, and the process started over again.

There were no safety inspectors on site. Stateside or in Japan, there were five safety inspectors per gun, with so much regulation that getting a round off every five minutes was difficult. But in Vietnam, we honed our skills to fire one round every twelve seconds.

I was assigned to be a powder man on Wendell's gun whenever a gunner had to go on OP duty. I'll explain this later.

Firing a 155mm gun was impressive. The gun crew consisted of the gunner, assistant gunner, powder man, and the person who controlled the quadrant for elevation. The gunner sighted the gun along the aiming stakes. The gun's turret could traverse fifteen degrees from center to either side. Anything more meant moving the whole gun and resetting the aiming stakes.

Rounds were high-explosive (HE rounds) and white phosphorus (WP rounds). They also fired flares that lit up the sky at night, using long and short powder bags. The range was determined by the combination of powder bags and the angle of the barrel. This information came from the FDC bunker. Communication wires and headsets were used to relay information.

When fired, the gun rose off the ground. The scarifier on the back resembled a large bulldozer blade with teeth, absorbing the recoil. Gun crews covered their ears and braced themselves for the noise and shock.

When commanded to "fire for effect," we could fire rounds every twelve seconds. There were two guns in our platoon, Number 1 and Number 2. I was on the Number 1 gun. We were good, but we never beat the Number 2 gun.

After a month on Hill 51, life became routine. There were two reasons we occupied that hill. First, Que Son Valley was a natural approach to Da Nang Airfield, and we blocked that approach. Second, the valley was a rice-growing area, and we provided security for the farmers to harvest their rice without the Viet Cong taxing or bothering them.

Most fire missions were H&I (Harassing and Interdiction). Two of the larger fire missions included one where we fired on several sampans in a river. Another—by far the most exciting—involved a reconnaissance unit that had infiltrated a Viet Cong base camp and was calling in rounds inside the camp. We had to be very careful about that one. The major frustration with these fire missions was that they never told us if we hit anything. It really angered us.

During one fire mission, a group of five Marines stood back and watched us. We couldn't figure out who they were. However, when we completed our mission, they approached us, wanting to shake our hands and express their gratitude. They were the recon team inside the VC base camp. They said we did a great job.

Baptism by Friendly Fire

I don't remember how long it was before it happened. It was quiet, with a few small unit actions with the grunts. Prisoners were brought in from time to time, and I'd check them out. This was my first look at real Viet Cong, little skinny guys, some with bandaged wounds.

One evening after chow, the OPs and LPs took up their positions. It was my night to be on the gun crew. Dark came, and we hit the sack; there was nothing else to do. In the bush, there were no lights after dark.

Having trained for rocket or mortar attacks, we had designated places to go so our officers and staff knew where to find us. Kevin, our Corpsman, and I were in the sandbagged water buffalo (water trailer).

During rocket or mortar attacks, the artillerymen manned their guns, firing back as rounds came in. It was better to fight back as soon as possible. The guns were given a pre-arranged set of coordinates to fire on. They were calculated areas where the enemy could set up artillery or rockets. Outgoing artillery was a familiar sound. Big booms didn't bother us; we slept right through them.

"INCOMING!! RED ALERT!"

Awake in a split second, I jumped into my boots, grabbed my flak jacket, helmet, and rifle, and ran to the sandbagged water buffalo. The world was blowing up around me. I could see and hear the explosions of the incoming rounds. Kevin was on the ground, snuggled up against the sandbags, face in the dirt. I followed suit, yelling at Kevin to check if he was okay.

Gary Jones was running around in circles right outside, yelling, "I CAN'T FIND MY HELMET!!!" Rounds landed everywhere, and we shouted for him to join us. He didn't know whether to go to his position or go back and look for his helmet. Kevin and I jumped up, grabbed him, and hauled him into our sandbagged area.

During a lull, the gun crew called out my name, needing a powderman. I grabbed my rifle and ran to the gun pit.

Halfway there, a salvo of rounds exploded around me. I saw a hole in the ground, jumped in, and lay there. But the gun crew kept yelling to get my ass over there. Jumping up, I realized I didn't have my rifle. I looked around but couldn't find it. The gun crew was screaming at me. As I ran to the gun, jumping over the berm, I tripped over my rifle thirty feet from where I'd hit the deck. Up on the tailgate, I took my position, not noticing that the incoming had stopped. Ready to ram home the first round, the cease-fire was called. I was to secure the gun. In total confusion, we asked each other what was going on. None of us knew.

Gunny asked for casualties. Kevin ran around checking on everybody. Thank God, everybody was accounted for. There were no casualties.

Unable to sleep the rest of the night, I was talking, trying to figure it out. Morning reports told us two were killed and twelve wounded, but no word of what had happened.

Gunny told us it was friendly fire. A platoon from 1st Battalion 3rd Marines was on a sweep and got lost in the night. Not knowing where they were or who we were, they called artillery on us. Battalion Gunny figured it was friendly fire because the rounds came in salvos, not walked in as the CV do.

He got on the radio, calling the surrounding hills that had artillery. Later, we heard that heads rolled because of that action, the platoon commander from 1/3 for getting lost, and the FDC officer who fired on us should have had our position plotted on their charts. Two marines were killed, and twelve were wounded.

The platoon from the 1/3 came into our compound to fly out. It's hard to imagine the vibes and hard looks we had toward those Marines in 1/3. Nobody spoke to them as they loaded up on the choppers.

Wondering about the hole I'd jumped into the night before. It was an indentation in the soft dirt where a deuce and a half truck had been the day before, unloading 155 rounds. Thinking I was secure below the surface, I'd lain on top, clasping my helmet, as rounds dropped around me. The rifle? I'd heaved it thirty feet when I hit the deck. Glancing down, I noticed the unpolished white toes of my jungle boots.

Civil Action Mission, Que Son Village

Anti-Tank Mines

Danny Dietrich and I were in the same fire team and gun crew, manning the same observation post (OP). He rode shotgun on my dozer when I was sent out on civil action missions.

Danny and I have stayed in contact over the years. He recently retired from a manufacturing plant that produces manufactured housing. The last time I visited him in Riverside, California, his wife recovered from a horrible traffic accident.

I received a mission to dig a dump for the villagers, so I picked up this little Vietnamese kid. We had met when Danny and I went to the village for a beer. Wearing oversized rubber boots, the kid had been kicking a dead rat down the street. Stopping our conversation, we invited him to one of the kiosks and bought him a Coke while we drank our beer. From then on, we were buddies.

Danny jumped off as I started digging, with the little kid sitting beside me. I had to dig eight feet deep. At four feet, the kid started yelling at me, slapping my back, and pointing to the rear of the dozer where a rocket lay on the ground.

Where the heck did that come from? Looking to the left, I saw I'd skimmed the side of a buried Viet Cong ammo cache. Rockets and anti-tank mines fell out, lying behind my dozer. I was getting ready to back over them when the kid pounded my shoulder.

Danny ran back to the compound to report our find and returned with a demolition officer. The officer told us to get out of there—the whole thing was wired up. Clearing and retrieving the cache required six loads on a small flatbed vehicle, commonly referred to as a mule.

That little kid saved our lives.

On Listening Post, Hill 51

On the outskirts of our compound, inside the wire, were outposts we call OPs, positioned 30 yards apart around the entire perimeter. Each OP had an M-60 machine gun with overlapping fields of fire from the OPs on either side. A communication wire connected them to the command post (CP) via a small handset for communication. Outside the OPs, around the perimeter, there were rows and rows of concertina barbed wire to keep out the enemy. A secret access route was established through the wire to facilitate movement in and out.

At night, infantry security patrols went 100 yards outside the wire and set up ambush sites. Just outside the wire sat a three-man listening post (LP). The men sat there all night listening for enemy infiltrators trying to sneak through the wire.

Wendell announced it was my turn to go out with him and Dave Orton on LP. But first, we had evening chow. We waited until dark before heading out.

I was assigned to man the hand-held radio. A radio operator would hit the mike button twice every hour on the hour to confirm the outpost was secure. The radio monitor would listen for the squelch sound and respond with two hits on his mike button. Otherwise, radio silence would be maintained unless we heard or saw enemy activity.

When darkness came, we saddled up with helmets, flak jackets, cartridge belts, extra ammo, grenades, and gas masks strapped to our thighs. Fully equipped, we followed the secret access route through the wire.

That first time on LP, I was nervous, to say the least. The access route consisted of a zigzag pattern of small openings between each row of wire. Going through them, it dawned on me that if we came under attack, there was no way in hell we'd make it back through in the dark. We'd have to fight it out the best we could from the outside.

Wendell wanted to set up our LP site on the other side of the Ly-Ly River, twenty-five meters out from our sector. Being gung-ho, he thought it would be a good idea to combine our LP task with an ambush site as well. He informed me our call sign was LP-7. Wendell had done this numerous times and was well acquainted with the terrain. Once we crossed the river, I was to contact the CP and inform them of our alternative position.

I'd feel a lot better if we stayed next to the wire.

Slowly making our way through the wire, we maintained a safe distance between each other. At the river, we crossed over one at a time. Wendell went first, then Dave, then me. It wasn't a particularly dark night, and we felt exposed as we crossed back over. We sat for a minute to listen, then I called in with a slight whisper to report on our position.

"CP, this is LP-7; come in."

I heard, "CP."

"LP-7 is in an alternative position."

"Wait one," came back.

Someone else got on the radio. A captain seemed agitated as he said, "LP-7, what is your alternative position?"

"On the other side of the river."

With more agitation in his voice, he said, "LP-7, there are reports of activity in our area. Get your asses back across the river and set up where you're supposed to. Is that understood?"

"Aye, aye, sir, LP-7 out."

Leaning over to Wendell, I whispered in his ear, "CP says to get our asses back across the river. There is a lot of activity in the area."

There was enough light to make out the disappointed look on his face as he stared at me. He was hoping for lots of activity, wanting to rack up a few kills.

After a pause, he said, "Okay, you are first. I'll bring up the rear."

Backtracking across the river, we settled in a spot ten feet in front of the wire. It was going to be a long night. Two of us would be on watch while one tried to sleep.

Sitting in one place the whole night on open ground in a tropical war zone had its problems. One problem was bugs. Lots of bugs of different types. These bugs wanted to eat you, take chunks out of your skin, and suck your blood. We constantly swatted, scratched, or slapped. Panic set in when something crawled under our clothes. Hell, or high water, couldn't stop our reaction to getting that critter off our bodies.

Always wet from high humidity, passing rain clouds, or sweat from the heat, a rash can occur in the crotch, armpits, or any part of the body where skin rubs together. That rash never went away. We kept a green towel around our necks to wipe the sweat from our eyes and face. It's a practice I still use today when working in hot conditions.

Sounds at night kept us alert. We didn't have to be trained for this—it came naturally. Sitting on LP was a miserable task. Our greatest hope was for the slight rays of dawn to make it through the wire to safety, still alive.

Dave was asleep. Wendell and I were on watch when we heard a noise to our left front, coming from some bushes. The hair on the back of my neck stiffened as I strained to hear and see something. It stopped. I relaxed, then heard it again. There was something there. A slight breeze blew in the direction of the bush, but the breeze wasn't causing the rustling.

Elbowing Wendell, I pointed to the bush. He heard it too. What he did next, I'll never understand. Taking a tear gas grenade, he pulled the pin and threw it into the bush.

Pulling the pin and throwing the grenade releases the safety handle, arming it. There's a five-second fuse before it ignites and releases tear gas. When the fuse blows, it sounds like a .45-caliber pistol going off.

The breeze brought the gas over our position. Instantly, we fought its effects—coughing, choking, unable to breathe or see. Gas got in our eyes, burning like hot coals. Tears streamed down our faces, mixed with mucus from our nostrils. It was a mad scramble for the gas masks strapped to our thighs. We were desperate to get them on and clear them so we could breathe again. We had trained for this situation in boot camp, though I'd hoped I'd never have to apply the training. It was no fun at all.

In Vietnam, at 2:00 a.m., the sound of a round being fired caused an instant alert. A Marine in the OP would grab his M-60 machine gun, put the butt of the weapon against his shoulder, place the trigger handle in his palm, put his finger on the trigger, and point the gun toward the noise.

Some Marines wouldn't hesitate to begin firing their 60-round belt of 7.62 ammo. Tonight, we were lucky. Communication sets were ringing, asking permission to fire.

With my gas mask on and my face cleared, I was able to get a couple of breaths of semi-clean air before the radio lit up. Immersed in a cloud of tear gas, I put the radio to my ear.

"LP-7, come in."

With the gas mask on, I couldn't answer, but I knew if I didn't respond, there was a good chance we'd get blown away by our own guys.

A more frantic call came in: "LP-7, COME IN. OVER!!"

I had to answer that call. I took two deep breaths from inside my gas mask and lifted it off my chin to answer the radio. Crying out under that gas cloud, I half-yelled, "HOLD YOUR FIRE, FOR GOD'S SAKE, HOLD YOUR FIRE!!" I added, "GAS!!"

I put the mask back on and cleared my throat, taking deep breaths. After the cloud of gas passed over, we took off our masks.

Dave looked at Wendell. "Jesus, Wendell, what the fuck?!"

Then he started laughing uncontrollably. The noise in the bush was a pig. It squealed and ran off when the grenade hit the bush.

Operation Swift - September 1967
Hill 51 - Que Son Valley

Operation Swift. I Am On The Left In The Gun.

Operation Swift should have been the scariest time of my life. But situations happened so fast and furiously that I didn't have time to get scared.

Dave and I were cleaning the gun over the motor hatches after a big fire mission the night before when we looked up and saw a Huey helicopter about a mile south, firing M-60s as it took a hit. A big white puff of smoke ascended as it went down. A few seconds later, the red flares went off: "RED ALERT!" The base became a madhouse of people running everywhere, grabbing weapons and ammo.

Gunnies were screaming at their Marines, rallying them together, and ensuring they had what was needed. The first group of 40 Marines moved out through the main gate, while the rest were getting organized and being issued supporting weapons, including M-60s, LAWs (Light Anti-Tank Weapons), 60mm mortars, and other equipment. We could hear small arms fire in the distance.

Dave and I ran to our hootch, grabbed our gear, and made it to the gun to get set up for a fire mission. On the gun, the crew were at battle stations awaiting orders.

Groups of Marines ran for observation posts (OPs), filling in the secondary line of defense as officers assessed the situation. The small arms fire was intensifying. The 105s began firing. The first group of Marines out was getting enveloped by the NVA, having to fight their way to the beleaguered security patrol. Small arms fire was getting closer, with tracers coming from their direction.

Gunny Snowman told us to stay at our stations awaiting further orders—we were taking over the OPs for the grunts going in support. The action was too close for us to take a shot. Kevin, our corpsman, was called to the command post. Numerous casualties were coming in. C Company, one of the first units out, took eighty percent casualties in twenty minutes after leaving the compound.

Choppers showed up in support, plus medevacs. The 105s were firing hot and heavy, and several of our Fire Direction Center boys went to help with ammo. The noise level was growing increasingly intense. Gun crews, including me, were standing by in frustration.

The first air strikes began—A-4s and Phantoms started coming in. Air strikes supporting Marines are a sight to behold. When we saw them, they were on the deck releasing napalm. There's nothing you can say about it—you stare in awe with your mouth hanging open. A jet would fly over, and there would be a massive increase in tracers as the NVA tried to shoot them down. The NVA had brought heavy anti-aircraft weapons mounted on wheeled carriages. It blew my mind that those jets didn't get shot down.

The sky was solid red with tracers.

As darkness set in, the battle was taking shape. We rarely knew what was going on in the big picture, so we did what we were told.

The battle shifted from the south, raging on both sides of our compound and moving toward the north. Our guys worked with the 105 howitzer crews or took over the OPs. Lieutenant Colonel Hilgartner tried to get in behind the NVA and push them our way, using Hill 51 as a blocking force with us and the tanks. Danny and I went to the perimeter wire to man an OP with an M-60 machine gun.

After dark, someone jumped into the hole with us. It was Chaplain Capodanno who told us it would be rough. I hadn't been scared until then. If the chaplain was coming around, you could bet you were going to be in tough shit. He visited briefly, then went on to the next hole.

Chaplain Capodanno was killed the next day while rescuing wounded Marines. He was one of nine chaplains in the Vietnam War who received the Medal of Honor. Ships and streets are named after him.

The NVA figured out what Hilgartner was doing, so the push to our compound never came. Later, the artillery personnel discovered that we were manning the entire compound alone.

Morning came. We sat in the OPs with the battle raging—choppers and jets everywhere, 105s and 155s pounding away. Grunts came in for a break to get hot chow. By now, elements of the 3rd Battalion, 5th Marines had entered the fight. All of 3/5 would be in it before it was over.

As I got chow and entered the mess tent, I saw a guy sitting there shaking like a leaf. His coffee cup went to his mouth, but he was shaking too much to drink. He was emotionally wasted, coming in from the field.

While I ate, this other guy pranced into the mess tent holding the barrel of his M-16 with the rest of it leaning over his shoulder. He was happy, whistling a tune as he came in. Looking at the shaking guy, he said, "Hey, Jones, what's the matter, man? Those VC can't shoot. They're shooting way high. Just stay low; you'll be all right."

I'm not sure if that comforted Jones.

The tanks took off. Hilgartner sent them to another ridge, pushing the NVA into a makeshift blocking force with tanks from Hill 63. The primary fight moved further up the valley, with plenty of action still going on around our compound. Late in the afternoon on the second day, the 105s ran out of ammunition.

Choppers flew in emergency runs of 105 rounds hanging from nets. Coming into the landing zone, they took hits from NVA anti-aircraft guns. At the LZ, we made a human chain to haul 105 ammo from the landing zone to the guns. It was night. I was in line, taking ammo and handing it to the next guy. The unbelievable noise of choppers coming in, artillery going out, everybody screaming and yelling. You couldn't hear anything.

Gunny came over and told me, "Means, start up your dozer and head to the CP."

At the command post, I met a captain who informed me that a CH-46 helicopter had taken a direct hit and dropped its ammunition basket in the rice paddy. Not wanting to leave it there, he sent out a rough terrain forklift to pick it up, but it got stuck in the mud. I was to get to the forklift, pull it out, find the basket, hook it up, and haul it in. I had no idea where this basket of ammo was.

The captain pointed in the general direction and told me to get going. I faintly saw the forklift stuck in the mud with a Marine sitting on top. I spun around, hooked up the forklift, and pulled it to the road.

I released the forklift and yelled, "Where's the ammo basket?"

He pointed at the way we had come and rushed back. Turning my dozer around, I looked for the basket of ammo as choppers flew in, dropping their loads.

As I crossed the paddy, a chopper must have gotten lost. I saw it coming near me. Then the pilot hit his landing lights and completely lit me up, and the ammo basket I was looking for when an NVA machine gun fired on the chopper. The pilot veered away, and I was a sitting duck. I went over, spun around, hooked it up, and started back, waiting to be plastered by the NVA machine gunner.

This fight lasted another week. 127 Marines were killed. I don't know how many NVA were destroyed—they were lying dead all over the place.

History proves that Operation Swift was one of the most critical operations of the war. The 1st Battalion, 5th Marines, got hit head-on by the 2nd NVA division, and the Marines stopped them in their tracks. A lot of good men died, and I knew quite a few of them.

We Won.

Ambushed at Tam Ky, Rvn '67

Army units of the 1st Air Cavalry took over Hill 51 in Que Son Valley while the Marines moved up to the DMZ. We left early in the morning to work our way to Hill 63 on Highway 1, then down to Chu Lai, where an LST waited to take us up to Da Nang.

Colonel Hilgartner had rotated out, and Major Thompson took over 1/5. Everybody was nervous about Major Thompson; our lives depended on him. It took some time to get accustomed to the new officers.

My dozer and I were first in line, so I could clear the way for the tanks and guns as we waited for the Cobra helicopter gunships to cover us from the air.

Grunts lay around with their gear, waiting for the command to move out. Our guns had a lot of weapons and gear piled up, along with C-rations and extra ammunition. Choppers had arrived the day before, hauling our excess gear to Chu Lai.

At 0800, the Cobra helicopters flew over, the Gunnies yelled, "All right, boys, saddle up, let's move out."

It was hotter than hell as the point moved out first, followed by the point squad, then the flankers. The main body began to move with grunts on either side of me. Tanks, guns, and rear security came last.

The road to Hill 63 was in a state of disrepair, and we knew it was mined. SOP (standard operating procedure) was to skirt the road and head through the rice paddies. I took off down the middle of the paddies, and everybody followed.

Everything went well until late in the afternoon, when we navigated through a ditch. It was no problem for the first tank and me; I kept going. After a while, I looked around. It was just me and the first tank. Where was everybody?

I looked at the tank driver and motioned, "What's up?"

He looked confused and shook his head. Returning, we found that the second tank had gotten stuck in the ditch, and the third tank was pulling it out.

The 1st Sergeant jumped up on my dozer, ordering me to build a ramp up to the road so the other tracked vehicles could get up. I tried to remind him that we weren't supposed to do that, but he said the orders came from the Major. I was confused because the tanks and guns could easily get up on the road without a ramp. However, I did what I was told, although I suppose not as well as I could have.

The next thing I knew, this guy came running full tilt toward me, jumped on my dozer, and chewed my ass off royally. It was Major Thompson. I can't remember the horrible names I was called, but he told me that when he ordered a ramp, he wanted a proper ramp.

I said, "Aye, aye, Sir," and made a nice ramp.

From then on, things went slowly. The gooks had dug big holes and stuck cut-up railroad iron in the road to make it unusable. I filled in holes and pushed these pieces of iron out of the ground, waiting to hit a mine at any time. The grunts were pissed—they wanted to get into Hill 63 before dark. They began to wonder about Major Thompson.

Late in the afternoon, we took sniper fire, with Cobras firing everywhere. Our flankers moved on a couple of hooches (thatched houses), blowing them up with M-79 grenade launchers. We were there for the night. Grunts formed a perimeter. It began to rain, then poured. Nothing happened the rest of the night.

Most of us slept only five minutes here and there, and we were wet and cold.

At first light, we moved out. I worked hard to get the road in shape for everybody else. A deuce-and-a-half truck blew up 100 yards down the road. Everybody waited while I pushed it off the road and filled the hole. When I returned, Hill 63 was only a click away—home free.

Moving out again, the tank behind me ran over a mine, blowing its track off. One grunt was so mad he threw the canteen he was drinking from into the rice paddy, cursing the shit out of Major Thompson. I realized I'd run over that mine five times and never triggered it.

We got into Hill 63 just in time for evening chow, and it started pouring again. The 9th Engineers had a flatbed waiting to pick up my dozer to take it to Chu Lai. I loaded it and then asked Captain Steen if I could ride in with the guns on Highway One. He permitted me, making me happy to stay with my buddies. It poured all night, so we found the best places to sleep we could. I didn't sleep much.

Tanks and guns fueled up in the night. We rearranged stuff to leave the first thing in the morning. Most of the grunts were airlifted out. A squad of 1/5 came with us for security.

The Ambush

We left at first light after early chow, heading down Highway 1 to Chu Lai. Two tanks led the way, followed by our two guns and a tank in the rear. The grunts piled on. I was riding on Mike Young's gun behind Wendell Shannon's gun, straddling the barrel and leaning back against the turret. Captain Steen rode on the same gun. Kevin, the corpsman, was riding on top of the turret on the first gun.

It was easy going compared to getting to Hill 63. The 9th Engineers were responsible for keeping the road open and safe, and it looked like they did a good job.

After traveling most of the day, we pulled into Hill 29, occupied by a Marine four-deuce outfit. The CO was a friend of Captain Steen's, and he wanted to pay a visit. They seemed happy to see us.

They had a deuce-and-a-half with a canvas covering the bed. Lifting the canvas, we found it filled with cases of Tiger Beer. Did that blow our minds! They began passing out beer. In a short time, we were shit- faced. It was a great place to take a break. How cool can it get? I couldn't figure out where they got that beer.

In the late afternoon, we staggered back to our vehicles, loaded up, and took off again. I was feeling pretty good despite being tired, wet, and cold.

Five miles from Tam Ky, Vietnamese people crowded the road. They waved with big smiles as we passed an ARVN compound (Army of the

Republic of Vietnam). Up the road, 200 meters away, rice paddies lined both sides, with the ARVN compound behind us. Two hundred yards across the paddy to our right was a village, with two small villages to our left just before a river.

A Huge Explosion!

The gun ahead of us blew up with Kevin on top of the turret. It ran over a buried culvert with a 400-pound charge in it. The detonating charge blew the 52-ton #1 gun off Highway One. Kevin went airborne along with the gun and landed on his back over the scarifier. I was sure he was dead. Gunny yelled at us to watch our heads as giant clods of dirt crashed down.

Concern for Kevin was short-lived as we took heavy small-arms fire. Tanks fired first. Wendell fired with the 50-caliber machine gun just over my head. Told to get off the gun and lay down a base of fire, I got up to jump. I was facing the ARVN compound and saw lots of muzzle flashes as rounds came our way.

I yelled at Wendell, "Incoming small arms at five o'clock!"

He turned the 50 on them, blowing them to shit. Jumping off the gun, I joined Lopez and Johnson, laying a base of fire at two small villages by the river. Dave Orton ran up to me in a panic, screaming that he couldn't hear—his eardrums blown out.

Vietnamese were caught in the crossfire and mowed down like dried grass. There was nothing we could do about it. We were fighting to gain fire superiority.

The guys were yelling for ammo as it got dark. I remembered a box of ammo on top of the gun. I yelled at Wendell that we needed ammo. Expecting he'd pass down bandoliers, in excitement, he pushed over the whole 50-pound box from the top of the gun. Standing there, I couldn't see as I reached to receive the ammo. The wooden box came flying down, crashing into my arms and face, nailing me in the chest. It knocked me to the ground. Cut up badly with blood streaming down my face, I lay there for a moment, trying to absorb the pain.

Cries for ammo continued. I struggled to get up, grabbed the box, and passed it out. Flares lit up the sky, marking a lull in the firing. We reloaded our weapons as incoming fire died down.

One parachute on a flare failed to open. It fell to the ground by the river, landing next to a man. He jumped up, becoming a perfect target for everybody on the line. We fired on this poor guy with every weapon we had. He was blown to pieces right before our eyes.

Standing there in awe, I felt somebody grab my shoulder and turn me around. I looked into the distorted face of Kevin, our corpsman. He was in such bad shape that he could hardly stand. I was sure he was dead. Somebody had noticed my bloody face and went and told him.

Struggling to get to me, he asked, "Bob, where are you hit? You, okay?"

I began to answer him when his eyes went blank, and he fell into my arms, then puked all over me and fell to the ground. We picked him up, took him over to the gun, and leaned him up against the track.

Dave Orton sat in the road, grasping his head, saying again, "We killed those people, we killed those people."

For years after the war, I tried to find Dave. I found out a few years back that he died in 1990 of acute alcoholism. Three of us visited his gravesite to give our final farewell.

A Medevac chopper came in and loaded up seven of our guys. Dave and Kevin were two of them. I stayed.

Wendell yelled at me to get on the 50-caliber machine gun because he needed to help short-track the blown-up gun. The rest of the night was quiet. I fired the weapon periodically to let them know we were awake.

At first light, the Vietnamese were pulling their dead out of the rice paddies. It was a sickening sight— small kids and mama-sans. Others just returned to work in their fields, going up and down the road like nothing had happened.

Orders came to start up the gun to take it back down the road, where engineers were coming to repair the hole in the road. Lopez and I were guarding the gun while everybody else was busy getting the other gun back on the road.

My face, arm, and chest throbbed.

The Vietnamese passed us on the road. A couple of kids put their hands up for food. C-rations were open on top of the gun, so I threw down a can to one of the kids. What a mistake! In an instant, we were surrounded by hundreds of Vietnamese begging for food.

"God!" I thought, "We just wiped-out half of these people's villages, and they have the balls to come begging for food!"

Two boys tried to get up on the gun. Pointing my rifle at them, I told them, "Di-di!" (go away). They backed off for a second, but the crowd kept getting closer. People laughed; more kids tried to get on the gun.

I was going to have to start shooting these people. I ran forward and kicked two boys in the chest, knocking them to the ground, to more screams of laughter. They kept coming. I didn't know what to do.

Grabbing brass .50-caliber casings on top of the gun, I heaved them as hard as I could, nailing people in their heads and chests. Grunts down the road saw we were in trouble and came running to clear the area.

Once the road was repaired, our gun and two tanks were ordered to go to Chu Lai. The rest would come as soon as they got the other gun up and running.

The Tam Ky bridge had been blown. The engineers had a ferry going across the river. It took an hour to get the vehicles across.

My face hurt as I peeled dried blood off my cheeks. Beat tired, with the night's adrenaline wearing off and three nights of practically no sleep, I saw a patch of grass by the side of the road. It'd be a great place to lie down for a minute. Dozing off, this little girl came up wanting to practice her English. I said something vulgar.

She was looking at me with eyes of fire, screaming at the top of her lungs, wagging her finger. "WHAT DO YOU TALK TO BABY-SAN LIKE THAT FOR?" She carried on for another minute, turned on her heels, put her nose in the air, and stomped off, hands on her hips.

Boy, did I feel like a heel.

Rolling into Chu Lai in the late afternoon, we went straight to the mess hall like a wild herd, weapons still in hand. Coming in from four months in the bush, we were in rough shape—nothing like these clean Chu Lai troops. Crowding at the front door, the first couple of guys stopped to figure out what to do. In the back, we pushed on, causing a lot of commotion. Inside, the mess hall went from a lot of chatter to dead quiet. We looked at them as they looked at us. The Chu Lai boys got out of line to give us their seats. It made us feel good.

Wild Ride in an Old LST

In the four months we were in-country, we took our guns to Que Son Valley, survived friendly fire, endured Operation Swift, were ambushed at Tam Ky, and maintained through hundreds of fire missions. No longer new guys, we looked and talked like battle-hardened Marines. The toes of our boots were worn white.

When the Marines moved north, the Army took everything between Da Nang and Chu Lai. We loaded everything on an old LST to go to Da Nang. This LST was contracted out to some Korean outfit to haul cargo and troops. It didn't have a number, just small black letters that said, "US Ship," no name. Korean civilians made up the crew.

Everything was loaded and dogged down. The ramp was raised, and the bow hatches closed. We backed off the beach. We were hungry, but the vessel had no working galley, so we opened C-rations in our troop compartment as the ship headed out to sea.

The ship began to roll heavily in the open ocean, cruising into a storm. "Typhoon" was mentioned. The vessel turned north, taking waves right on the bow, which rose high out of the water and then plowed into the next massive wave.

Several of us went out on deck to see what was happening. An active-duty naval ship wouldn't let us go out in such conditions, but this civilian crew didn't care what we did.

Lopez, Johnson, Don Lohnes, Bill Tinney, and I watched the Korean captain on the bridge perform some Asian exercises. Laughing, we focused on the huge waves crashing over the bow.

In the forecastle, a larger wave came over the bow about four feet off the deck. It seemed possible to get under the coaming when the wave crashed over and not get wet.

A plan took shape. From the forward hatch, as the ship rose, we ran forward to the coaming. We could perfect our timing so that the last man secured the hatch in plenty of time. With the ship rising, we lifted our hands in the air, shouting and screaming, yelling at the ocean to get us as the ship began its downward fall. It was chicken time—who'd be the last guy to duck under the coaming before the wave crashed over us?

Ducking under the coaming at the last second, tons of water rushed over us, but nobody got wet. The ship began to rise. We jumped up and howled, shouted, and carried on like flaming fools.

It was great fun. After three or four times, Bill wasn't coming up. He lay on the deck groaning in agony, green with seasickness, puking his guts out. Bill was a big guy, and he wasn't moving. We had to get him inside.

"Bill, we're going back in."

He said he couldn't get up. He was too sick. He puked again.

We needed a plan to get Bill inside. Lopez would go first as the ship rose, open the hatch, get inside, and secure it before the water got in. In the next wave, the three of us would drag Bill to the hatch, and Lopez would open it, allowing us to enter.

The time came. Lopez ran, opened the hatch, and got in. Next wave—we took hold of Bill, dragging him over the deck as he groaned. We reached the hatch as the ship was in its descent. Why wasn't it open? What was Lopez doing?

Frantically pounding on the hatch, we yelled for Lopez to open it. There were only seconds left before the crashing wave washed over the deck, potentially maiming or killing us. Bill was sure to drown. The hatch opened just as the water overflowed the coaming. Desperately, we pushed and rolled Bill in, jumping on top of him. Lopez and others pushed the hatch shut. There wasn't enough time to secure it as four feet of water rushed past. We held it the best we could. Bill lay at the bottom of the pile, groaning and puking.

Someone turned to Lopez and shouted, "Lopez! What the hell were you doing?"

Looking at us sheepishly, he admitted, "The handle got stuck. I couldn't get it open."

We tried to get Bill up to his rack in our compartment, but he was too big and sick.

Gunny came in and said, "Who's out on deck?"

"Nobody, Guns," we answered.

"The captain said somebody was out there. He wanted everybody inside."

"Okay, no problem."

Gunny noticed Tinney lying on the deck and asked, "What's wrong with Tinney?"

"Seasick, Gunny."

"Well, get him up in his rack."

"Tried, he won't go."

Gunny said, "Oh," and turned to leave the compartment

68 Tet, Bridge Ramp, Da Nang

Major battles took place at Hue, Saigon, Da Lat, and other cities during the 1968 Tet Offensive. However, beyond these headline engagements, there were hundreds of smaller firefights in which individual soldiers and Marines banded together to stay alive and defeat the enemy. My story is one of those engagements. This was also around the time I became a corporal.

After a wild ride through a typhoon from Chu Lai, we landed at the Bridge Ramp in Da Nang. Offloading from the rusty old LST, we traveled through Dog Patch around Liberty Hill, out to Red Beach, twelve miles north of Da Nang. Upon arrival at Red Beach, I immediately got to work with my dozer, building gun and ammo pits and constructing a large berm around our area.

At Red Beach, 1/7 (1st Battalion, 7th Marines) and a Marine engineer outfit were positioned south of us. The 1/7 provided perimeter security for the entire Da Nang area and ran numerous operations out in Happy Valley. Our guns provided cover fire for them whenever needed.

Red Beach was comparatively civilized after what we'd been through. A 105-artillery outfit was stationed next to us. They'd been there a while and had established a proper mess hall with Vietnamese workers. Real meals again, served on metal trays with silverware, were a treat.

I started making supply runs for the mess hall four times a week. I'd pick up one of the cooks, and we'd drive into Da Nang for foodstuffs at various locations.

Once, a little kid jumped on the truck and grabbed our frozen strawberries. The cook chased him, but the kid got away—no strawberries for us.

We took time off and went to China Beach for in-country R&R. As a Southern California surfer, I took advantage of the waves and got in some body surfing. A few Red Cross round-eyed girls were on the beach. We hadn't seen anything like that in a while. They weren't particularly pretty, but those round eyes made all the difference.

Operations became routine: a few harassment and interdiction fires at night, occasional daytime missions, driving for the mess hall, or cleaning our equipment.

We traded our M-14s for M-16s. Using my dozer, I built a small range to sight in our new rifles and set up targets. A natural competition developed to see who the best shot was. It was fun and broke the monotony. I outshot Gunny Snowman, which pissed him off.

We received a fire mission from an ARVN operation that appeared to be significant. However, after four rounds, they aborted the mission. The next day, a large investigation team arrived. We went over the entire mission with them. The atmosphere was tense, with a heavy weight in the air. It appeared we'd missed our target, and our rounds had landed on a doctor's house, killing his four daughters.

I never found out for sure what happened. One of our officers was transferred somewhere, and we never saw him again. Scuttlebutt was that an ARVN colonel had called in the mission because the doctor owed him money from a gambling debt and wouldn't pay up.

For Christmas, we went to see Bob Hope and Ann Margaret. Even though we were sitting so far from the stage that they looked like specks, it was a great show, and we appreciated it. If God allows anyone to live forever, Bob Hope should be one, and Ann Margret the other.

One day, Lt. Wasson told me to get a jeep. He wanted pictures to show his wife during his R&R in Hawaii. We took off for Liberty Hill, where there was a huge PX. Just before we arrived, we turned right and went out behind the mountain. Out in the countryside, we sped down a dirt road, stopping occasionally at a Catholic church and once in a small village surrounded by kids. Lt. Wasson would jump out and snap away with his camera. We had no idea the Tet Offensive was only a week away.

Strange things began happening that should have tipped us off that something was brewing. Someone must have known trouble was coming because they brought in two How 6s (Amtracs with small turrets mounting sawed-off 105mm guns). I helped set them up. They also added several more observation posts around our area. Lopez and I manned one of them. Late one night, I looked up at the mountainside and saw the flare of rockets.

Rocket attack! The rockets would flare for a few seconds, then glide silently the rest of the way in. It was terrifying to know that in moments, the world was about to explode. Lt. Wasson jumped up on top of the How 6 and started directing fire at the hillside. After the fifth round, the hillside exploded.

There was a huge cheer, as if our home football team had scored a touchdown. The next morning, Gunny organized a squad from our unit to sweep the area. We found blown-up equipment and unused rockets.

Lt. Wasson should have received a medal for exposing himself to incoming rockets and destroying that rocket position. Instead, he got reprimanded for not requesting permission first. It was a pretty shitty deal.

Lt. Wasson left the Marines after the Vietnam War. He and his wife moved to Oklahoma City and entered the oil and gas business. I visited him there, and they took me out to dinner at the Cattleman's Restaurant. He ran for the state legislature as a Democrat and lost.

***

Two nights later, about a mile down the road, the Popular Forces (PF) compound run by Army Special Forces came under attack. It was one hell of a fight. Two companies from 1/7 went down the road in a deuce-and-a-half and unloaded right next to us to join the battle. How 6s and 105s were firing like crazy. We fired our rifles at two tree lines. The PF compound was overrun entirely, but the Marines from 1/7 eventually flushed out the enemy. These were preemptive strikes before the real thing. Our supposedly secure Red Beach compound had turned into a genuine hellhole.

Lt. Wasson left for R&R, and Capt. Steen was transferred to Khe Sanh to direct artillery.

Capt. Steen served in the Marines for thirty years. When he retired, he moved to Florida and worked selling software. We play golf twice a year just south of Jacksonville. He and Judy insist I stay with them in their home whenever I visit.

With no officers present, Gunny Snowman received orders to saddle up—we were moving north to an unknown destination. The guns went overland via Highway 1 through Hai Van Pass. I was sent with my dozer to the Bridge Ramp to wait for a Landing Craft Utility (LCU) to transport me to Phu Bai. From there, the 9th Engineers were supposed to haul me out to Camp Evans. I had less than two weeks left in-country before our rotation home.

After unloading my dozer, I checked in with the Navy Chief Seabee in charge of the bridge ramp. He was expecting me and told me to grab something to eat from the lunch truck and wait. The LCU is scheduled to arrive around 1500 hours.

The time came and went, but there was still no LCU. By 1700, there was still no boat. I asked the Chief if he knew when it was coming. He didn't know what was going on but told me to wait. Fifteen Army guys were waiting for the same LCU.

As darkness fell, the Seabees secured everything and returned to their compound. I sat on my dozer, realizing it was going to be a long night. As I hunkered down trying to sleep, we suddenly came under attack. Small arms fire erupted from nowhere, with rounds flying in from upriver.

I leaped off my dozer and lay face down in the dirt. The Army guys positioned by a nearby wall were returning fire. I picked myself up and ran over to help, asking one of the soldiers what I should do. He just stared at me.

I could see muzzle flashes down by the river and started firing back. There was some light from the city, but down by the water, it was pitch-black, except for the muzzle flashes. I emptied four magazines, firing at the flashes. If we had been overrun, I would have been screwed. I remembered seeing an ammo palette earlier and left the firing line to look for it. I grabbed a box and returned to my dozer and reloaded my magazines. A few rounds were still flying around, but the situation was calming down at our location. Looking across the city, I could see tracer fire and hear gunfire mixed with explosions. This wasn't supposed to happen in Da Nang—not with only a few days left in-country. Was I worried? You bet I was.

I stayed by my dozer for the rest of the night. With my time so short, they could get me if someone needed me. I felt helpless, with no idea what to do. I was utterly alone. As far as I could tell, nobody knew what was happening or that I was even there. I didn't know who to turn to for directions or help.

***

The fighting continued throughout the night around Da Nang. It was the first night of the 1968 Tet Offensive. At first light, the Seabees arrived and inquired about the situation.

"You tell me," I replied.

Where was the LCU? He didn't know. Looking down at the water, I could see bloated bodies slowly swirling in an eddy. The chow truck showed up, and I went to get something to eat.

The Seabee said, "How can you eat with those dead bodies floating there?" I answered with a smile—I was starving.

The rest of the morning was chaos. Nobody knew anything. The Seabees told me to hang tough while they tried to figure out what was happening.

Back at my dozer, something strange occurred. While trying to figure out how to contact anyone, I looked toward town. At the end of a block with a sidewalk and an eight-foot cement wall, I saw ten armed figures running around the corner and stopping. What blew my mind was that they appeared to be wearing Hawaiian shirts. Confused by this surreal situation, I watched them suddenly run toward the opposite corner. They were bunched up, so when the lead man stopped abruptly, those behind him, not paying attention, plowed into them, knocking each other down. It was like something from a Keystone Cops movie. This pile of bodies in Hawaiian shirts struggled to get up, then ran back the way they came.

Years later, it dawned on me that they were NVA wearing camouflage shirts. Camouflage uniforms weren't introduced to U.S. forces until after I got out. I knew the NVA was using them in some areas, but I'd never seen them until that moment.

Late in the afternoon, a company of ARVN troops arrived and took up positions around the bridge ramp. The lunch truck had left that morning and never returned, leaving me to wonder where I would get something to eat. The Seabees had no answers.

The entire country was in complete pandemonium. I could hear firefights in the distance. My situation was obviously way down on the priority list. As darkness fell, the Seabees packed up and left me with the company of ARVN and twenty Army guys.

***

It happened again that night. Rounds came from everywhere. The ARVN fired every weapon they had. I stayed with my dozer, figuring if we got overrun, I'd fight it out from there.

In the morning, I was still alive, with eleven days left in-country, wondering if anybody even knew I was there. I was confused and scared.

The Seabees arrived in the morning with the information. The LCU wasn't coming—the landing ramp we were headed to had been overrun. The Chief said eleven Seabees were dead. He gave me a phone number to call the 13th Marines.

A lieutenant Colonel answered. I told him I was Corporal Means at the bridge ramp with my dozer from 5th Guns. I'd been trying to get my dozer to Phu Bai to catch up with my unit when all hell broke loose. We'd been hit the last two nights, the LCU wasn't coming, and I was starving.

Then I said, "Colonel, I've got eleven days left in-country. What do you want me to do?"

"Wait right there," he replied.

I heard the jeep coming before I saw it. Weapons bristle from every angle. It screamed into the bridge ramp and stopped at my dozer.

The colonel looked at me from the passenger seat and asked, "Are you, Corporal Means?"

"Yes, sir."

"Grab your gear and get in."

"Sir, what about my dozer?"

"Fuck your dozer. Get your ass in here."

He took me to the MAG (Marine Air Group) 16 airstrip and handed me a set of orders to catch a Caribou aircraft to Phu Bai. From there, I was to catch a C-123 to Dong Ha, then another plane to Quang Tri, and ask for directions to Camp Evans.

As we arrived, the Caribou was loaded with troops. I saluted and said, "Thank you, sir." He returned the salute, wished me good luck, and drove off. Ten minutes later, I was airborne.

At Phu Bai, the C-123 took off over the water. As we approached land, the crew chief put on his flak jacket, and the plane descended steeply. An Army staff sergeant thought we were going to crash and panicked. The crew chief grabbed him, yelled something in his ear, and he settled down. Once over land, flying only a few feet off the ground at full throttle, I looked up through the portholes and could see treetops.

Approaching Dong Ha, the plane regained altitude, made a sharp left turn, and landed. Upon touchdown, the pilot threw both engines into reverse, rapidly slowing us down with only a loose strap to hold us in place. The plane didn't stop rolling. We ran off while others ran on, as mortars began dropping on the airstrip. Directed to a bunker, we ran like hell. The C-123 took off immediately.

I heard my name called to board another Caribou with engines running. In Quang Tri, an Army staff sergeant stood there, clipboard in hand. I asked how to get to Camp Evans. He told me to go down the road for two clicks until I saw an LZ on the right. When a chopper came in, I should ask the crew chief if he was going to Camp Evans; eventually, I'd get a ride. I took off running, desperate to get back to my unit.

The third chopper that landed was going to Camp Evens. They took off, staying right on the deck and flying as fast as they could.

Camp Evans had 101st Airborne troops everywhere. Not seeing our guns, I asked an Army guy driving a mule if he knew where they were. He told me to hop on, and he'd take me there. I approached the CP tent just as Gunny Snowman was coming out. We looked at each other.

He spoke first: "Means, where the fuck have you been?"

I was too exhausted to answer.

He took my rifle and told me to get something to eat, get cleaned up, and hit the rack. I did precisely that, falling asleep before my head hit the pillow. When I woke up, my rifle was lying against the rack, spotless.

Gunny Snowman was a friend until he passed away three years ago.

Camp Evans was a massive base, and Tet was raging everywhere. The men who had come over with the guns were ready to head back home.

The 2nd Battalion, 5th Marines, battled it out in Hue City. The 1st Air Cavalry Division at Camp Evans was supposed to be airlifted behind Hue as a blocking force for the Marines. Late that afternoon, the Army brought in twenty helicopters for an early morning airlift the next day.

During the night, we were woken by "Red Alert!" I was too tired and emotionally drained to take refuge in a bunker. I didn't think I was going to survive Vietnam anyway.

Through a flap in the tent, I watched mortars walk down the row of helicopters, blowing them up one by one. Several Army personnel were killed.

The 1st Air Cav never made it to Hue. The Marines paid a terrible price.

Gunny told me he'd extended for another six months and wouldn't be going home with us. The new replacements had arrived, and we were ready to leave.

Somehow, the Navy had gotten my dozer to the Perfume River, and I had to retrieve it. The last thing I wanted to do was pick up my dozer in Hue. I would have been pleased to leave it at the bridge ramp in Da Nang.

Tinney, Lohnes, Kevin, and I took a jeep to load my dozer on a flatbed truck. On our return trip, we heard an explosion and saw a black mushroom cloud ahead of us. We came upon a civilian bus that had hit a mine—dead civilians were scattered everywhere. A dead baby lay in the road, its arms and legs reaching toward the sky. We stopped and got out. Kevin went down the embankment to where an ARVN soldier was holding a woman, her intestines spilling out. He knelt as the ARVN held up a dirty, torn bandage, motioning for Kevin to wrap it around the woman. Kevin went catatonic, staring at her in silence. I went down, grabbed him, and pulled him back to the jeep. There was nothing we could do, and I wanted to go home. Kevin was never the same after that.

The next day, we loaded onto choppers back to Quang Tri, then took a C-123 to Da Nang with a plane full of body bags containing dead Marines. I spent two days there, processing out at a Seabee compound. They had a bar where I got so drunk I fell off my stool and had to be dragged back to my hooch. We stayed completely shit-faced the entire time. With horrible hangovers, we loaded onto a C-130 for a sixteen-hour flight back to Okinawa.

***

We went to Camp Hansen for three days, spending most of our time at the Animal Pit (an enlisted men's club), trying to figure out how to get to Kin Village for some female companionship. While there, I witnessed thirty fights at the Animal Pit.

We pulled out our green uniforms, had them cleaned, and put them on with our combat ribbons. We then stood in inspection before being taken to Naha Air Base to board a Continental Airlines 707. It was unbelievable. The stewardesses were beautiful. I was convinced we'd never make it home alive. We landed in Hawaii to refuel, then continued to El Toro.

My mother, sister Susan, and her husband, Gary, were there to greet me. I had thirty days of leave coming, then I was to return to Camp Pendleton with nine months of service remaining.

Back in the USA

Back in the USA

As an engineer, the Marines assigned me to artillery with Hotel Battery, 3rd Battalion, 13th Marines, stationed at Camp Los Pulgas in Camp Pendleton, California. Being a short-timer, I was marking time waiting for my discharge. I never contemplated reenlistment.

After a week at my new duty station, we received orders to participate in an amphibious assault exercise—the last thing I wanted to do after a year of combat in Vietnam. We loaded our gear into trucks, drove down to San Diego, loaded everything onto an old LSD ship, and attacked the California beaches via landing craft. We spent ten days traipsing around the hills of Camp Pendleton with no showers or hot food.

Returning to our barracks, my platoon leader approached me and asked if I'd fill a billet in a lifeguard course at the local pool. I accepted instantly.

The four-day course was a breeze; I passed with flying colors. It allowed me to meet the pool staff. Mike was the NCOIC and head instructor. We hit it off well, and I spent my free time with the pool crew, swimming, and playing tennis on the court next to the pool parking lot.

After receiving my lifeguard certificate, I returned to my outfit, where I worked in the motor pool with the motor transport people, performing maintenance on my dozer and helping wherever needed.

Two weeks later, I was approached again—this time to take a WSI (Water Safety Instructor) course. Whoever took the course needed a lifeguard certificate, and I was the only one in the battalion who had one. This course lasted a week.

I had no problem earning the WSI certificate. With both certificates qualifying me to work at the pool, I approached Mike for a job.

Mike didn't have an opening but mentioned that a Drown Proofing Instructor (DPI) position was coming up. If I could get my DPI certificate, he'd try to get me the job. Surprisingly, a week later, I was asked to take the DPI course down in San Diego at MCRD. The DPI candidate needed both a lifeguard certificate and WSI certification—I was the only person in the battalion with both. Off I went for the two-week course.

Drown-proofing is a technique developed by Fred Lanoue, utilizing natural body buoyancy, along with relaxation and breathing techniques, to keep a person afloat for extended periods until rescue. The Marine Corps adopted this technique due to its amphibious mission, requiring Marines to pass a drown-proof course before deploying overseas.

The two-week course was intense. The instructors pushed us hard, requiring us to swim underwater twice the length of an Olympic-size pool and stay afloat for two hours with our hands and feet tied behind our backs.

It sounds grueling and dangerous, but with proper training, it can be effective. Surviving for long periods in the ocean builds confidence around water. I passed the course feeling good about my accomplishment.

When I reported back to my unit with my certificate, I went to the pool to talk to Mike. He was excited I'd passed and told me the DPI opening was available. He directed me to Battalion S3 to see the Gunny for placement.

I made an appointment with the S3 Gunny, but for some reason, he refused to give me the job. When I asked if anyone else in the battalion was qualified for this position, he informed me that he was not aware of anyone. That didn't persuade him. I think he just wanted to be difficult. I was determined to get that job and finish my Marine Corps tour as a DPI.

My only option was to request Captain's Mast and go over the S3 Gunny's head. So close to the end of my enlistment, I wasn't going to miss this opportunity.

Requesting Captain's Mast is part of naval tradition. When someone of a lesser rank has a complaint against someone of a higher rank, they can go directly to the captain and state their case without informing the rest of the chain of command. The problem is that others in the chain become nervous, not knowing what you're taking before the captain, so they try to find out about your issue and whether it involves them.

I had good reason and was going for broke. After three and a half years in the Marine Corps, I was familiar with my rights and didn't want anyone to get in my way or try to dissuade me from getting that job. I spent the rest of the day polishing my boots, polishing the brass belt buckle on my white canvas utility belt, laying out a freshly starched utility uniform, and starching a well-worn but spotless cover.

When requesting mast, it's necessary to look exceptionally squared away and follow military procedure to the letter. Otherwise, it could spell big trouble. You never went before the captain haphazardly.

I showed up for formation at 0800, looking my best and totally squared away. Usually, we only squared away enough to pass general inspection, so my guys wanted to know what was going on, but I didn't tell them.

After formation and roll call, I went to the platoon's Staff Sergeant and informed him that I was requesting a Captain's Mast.

Looking blankly at me, he said, "What for?"

"I want to see the captain."

As expected, that made him nervous. He asked if there was anything he could do for me. I told him no, I wanted to see the captain. From there, it went to my platoon commander, a 2nd Lieutenant. When my platoon Sergeant said to him that Corporal Means was requesting Captain's Mast, I'm sure this was the Lieutenant's first such request. He got nervous too, put his hand on my shoulder, and asked if there was anything he could do to help.

"No, Sir. I want to see the captain."

He asked if I wanted the day off to think about it. He took his car keys out of his pocket and offered to let me take his car and relax for the day.

"No, Sir, I want to see the captain."

He took me to the 1st Sergeant to make an appointment. The 1st Sergeant entered the captain's office, came out, and told me to return at 10:30; the captain would see me then.

At 10:20, I re-entered the company office, confident I'd get that job at the pool.

At precisely 10:30, the captain yelled, "Corporal Means, front and center."

I marched into the captain's office, executed a left face, took one step, executed a right face, snapped my heels together, came to full attention facing the captain, looked straight ahead, and stated, "Sir, Corporal Means reporting as ordered, Sir!"

"At ease, Marine, have a seat," he said, pointing to a chair next to his desk. "Corporal Means, what can I do for you?"

"Sir, there's an opening at the pool for a drown-proof instructor, and I'm the only person in the battalion qualified for this position. I went to the Gunny at S3 and asked for the job, but he refused. Sir, the Marine Corps spent $4,000 training me for this position, and that Gunny won't give me the job. I want to know why."

For the next three minutes, he chewed me out for not coming to him first. Then he ordered me to go with him, and we marched over to the S3 office.

The captain asked, "Gunny, is there an opening at the pool for a DPI?"

"I don't know, sir, let me look," the Gunny responded, opening a book. "Yes, Captain, it seems there is."

"Is there anybody else in the battalion other than Corporal Means qualified to fill that position?"

"No, sir, there doesn't seem to be."

In a forceful voice: "Put Corporal Means down to fill that billet."

"Aye, aye, Sir."

I got the job. A week later, I received orders to report to the pool and serve under Sergeant Mike for pool duty. I'd pulled it off.

When I checked in, Mike was getting ready to take unauthorized leave for a diving trip to Baja, Mexico. He explained how things worked: "We have no DP classes for two weeks. We take off all we want. You need to be available by phone, and if anyone calls for you, we will inform them that you're at the Main side and will return in the morning. We call you, and you haul ass back here to report the next day."

Then he loaded his bag in his car, leaving the number where he could be reached on the desk.

As he was leaving, I asked, "What do you want me to do?"

"Hang out and answer the phone." Then he was gone.

Two other people were assigned to the pool. They were both Navy corpsmen, nowhere to be found. I was at the pool for three days before anybody showed up.

On the third night, somebody came stumbling in, totally drunk, banging into things and making a real racket. Cursing his head off, he woke me up. I got out of my rack and asked what was going on. In his drunken stupor, he looked at me and said, "Who the fuck are you?!"

I said, "I work here," which caught him off guard.

He replied, "I work here too."

He climbed into a rack and passed out. I went back to bed, thinking we'd work it out in the morning.

The pool facilities included a small squad bay with six racks, a head and shower, an office, and a small kitchen with refrigerator, stove, and sink. There was a larger area with a bigger head and a shower for trainees. Around the pool deck was a high concrete wall, and at the deep end stood a thirty-five-foot tower. Next to that were a high diving board and a regular diving board. On the side were bleachers where we instructed Marines in drown-proofing. For recreation, chaise lounges were scattered around for people to sit in, and there was a tennis court outside the front door. It was open for use during weekends and after hours when one of us was on lifeguard duty, in case anybody showed up, but nobody ever did.

Up early, I made coffee and went out to the pool deck, wondering what to do for breakfast. I hadn't been there long when the other guy came stumbling out, asking if there was any coffee.

"Sure, in the pot."

He grabbed a cup and joined me on the pool deck, introducing himself. He asked how I'd got there, so I told him my story while we enjoyed our coffee.

He was a Navy corpsman who hadn't been shipped overseas. When they sent him to the fleet, they stuck him at the pool where he'd been for six months due to his DPI qualification.

***

When Mike returned, he familiarized me with his instruction techniques. Classes were made up of 20 Marines who didn't want to be there. They had to pass this course. Mike was motivated and had put together a professional program. He gave a lecture on Fred Lanoue's drown-proofing techniques from a historical perspective and explained how this could save your life. He went through the method itself, using me to demonstrate on dry land—the dead man's float, with the head in the water, and total relaxation.

After the land drills, everybody went into the pool to practice what they'd learned. Ten percent were sinkers; they went straight to the bottom. We taught the sinkers the travel stroke. In real-life situations, we figured they wouldn't make it, but they received the basics.

The 35-foot tower simulated jumping off the side of a sinking ship. On top of the tower, I demonstrated the jump position: put one hand on my crotch, hold my nose with the other, then jump feet first into the pool. Occasionally, I did a backflip off the tower to add color to the routine. Mike acted pissed off and told me to get back up there and do a proper entry. I'm sure the sinkers wondered what was going on.

Marines jumped in fully clothed with their boots. When they made it to land, they would need boots. After clearing the impact area, they'd slowly remove their boots, tie the bootlaces together, hang them around their necks, and then proceed with the DP technique.

To pass the course, they had to stay in the water for one hour. Twenty percent didn't make it and had to come back until they passed.

During the test, I'd be on the lower diving board wearing sweatpants, flip-flops, a T-shirt, and a Marine cover, with a whistle around my neck.

One of our crew members was on top of the tower, and another was on the opposite side of the pool. Mike was at the bleachers teaching the sinkers the travel stroke.

I yelled loudly, "First three to the edge of the tower. Take jump position. Ready... JUMP!"

We watched to make sure they came to the surface. If they took too long coming up, one of us dove in to check on them. Sometimes, we would take them to the side of the pool and ask if they wanted to continue. Most did because they didn't want to do this again.

One young black Marine slipped through the cracks. He stood on the edge of the tower as instructed, took the jump position, and jumped on command. Hitting the impact area, he went straight to the bottom. The instructor on the tower and I watched when he did not come up.

I turned to Mike and said, "Hey Mike, this guy isn't coming up."

Mike came over to the side of the pool, looked down, and said, "Yes, he is, don't worry about him," then went back to his lecture.

Watching a little longer, I kicked off my flip-flops, sweatpants, shirt, and cover, saying, "MIKE... This guy ain't coming up!!!"

Mike came and looked: "He's coming up, goddamn it! Leave him alone."

I couldn't wait any longer. The instructor on the tower and I dove in after him. He sat on the bottom with his legs and arms folded, calmly looking up at me. He was a passive victim. I reached down, grabbed him under the right armpit, and took him to the side of the pool.

I said to him, "What in the hell were you thinking?!"

With a big smile, he replied, "I wanted to jump off that tower. I knew you'd be down to get me sooner or later."

I sent him to the sinkers class.

Los Pulgas beach had a great surf break. I loaded up my surfboard and traveled down to surf the morning glass-off. I had the beach to myself. It was part of the Marine base, and only Marines were allowed there.

After surfing, I have chow and wait for the afternoon class, then play tennis until dark. There wasn't a better job in the Marine Corps: three DP classes a week, and other than that, we were on our own.

I grew my hair long, wondering if I was still in the Marines. I discovered I was getting a ninety-day cut on my enlistment, so the Marines could save money on not having to feed me. Life was good, but I was eager to get out and become a civilian again. I didn't know what I was going to do, but I didn't care.

Herbie showed up and checked into the pool. Herbie was recovering from his wounds from Vietnam, so they put him there for light duty. He was from Orange County, where he went on weekends. He liked to surf, joining Paul and me on our morning surf trips.

Herbie asked if I wanted to go to Orange County for the weekend—he needed a ride. I'd bought a blue MGB sports car with my Vietnam money. On Friday night, we took off in my car to Orange County to attend a party with many of Herbie's civilian friends.

Herbie's best friend was Larry Morgan. Larry had just gotten out of the Army and lived with his parents. His dad was a WWII vet who got his legs blown off in his tank in France. Larry's dad had a high-ranking job at the Long Beach shipyard and had a heart for Vietnam vets—he included us in the family. Larry's place became our weekend home. I plugged into this clique of counterculture people: drugs, lots of high school and college girls. They knew how to party, and I was into that.

I became a Sergeant ten days before my discharge date. To celebrate, I went to the mess hall for lunch because the Sergeants went directly to the head of the line. I wanted to do that once.

Discharge day came unceremoniously. Three days before my discharge, I was called back to my unit to turn in my gear and sign the necessary paperwork. My hair had grown long, and not wanting any trouble, I went to the barber and had it cut.

I was called into the CO's office for a chat. The command had changed, and I'd never met this new Captain. He'd tried to get me back after he took command, but was refused due to the short time remaining and my duties at the pool. He shook my hand, wished me luck, then sent me over to the battalion for my final papers.

I walked into an office where a few other Marines were waiting for their discharges. A 2nd Lieutenant told me to sign a paper and said I was free to go. Not even a thank you.

That was it. I got in my MGB and drove off the base to my mother's house in Garden Grove, not knowing where to go from there. I spent a week with her.

Sex, Drugs, and Rock & Roll

Herbie, still in the Marines but soon to be discharged, visited on weekends with Larry and me to go surfing. Larry had spent his tour in Vietnam as a mail clerk in Saigon with the Army.

Herbie served with Amtracs. During an NVA rocket attack, Herbie's Amtrac took a direct hit. A rocket landed squarely on his vehicle, killing his radio operator and severely wounding Herbie. He was rescued barely alive and flown to Japan for a long recovery, teetering between life and death.

We often talked about our time in Vietnam. Herbie told me the only thing that kept him alive was his desire to see his wife back in California. The day he returned to the States, she served him divorce papers.

I destroyed my MGB driving it like a Formula One race car, then sold it to a dealer for $1,500 and bought an old BSA 250 single-cylinder motorcycle. It was a classy old bike, though somewhat heavy. After surfing, I'd take it down to the riverbed for dirt riding, making wild jumps over hilly terrain. Meeting other dirt bikers there, I was introduced to the Yamaha 250 DT1 two-stroke. Those bikes amazed me. I had to get one.

Herbie joined me on dirt bike rides. When I mentioned wanting one of those Yamahas, he offered to buy my BSA. I sold it to him for $200, and that same day, I purchased a new Yamaha. I loved that bike so much I couldn't stay off it.

On a deserted street, I challenged Herbie to a race, confident my hot DT1 would crush that BSA. We raced five times, and each time Herbie edged me out by a length.

Herbie loaded his backpack, filled the BSA's fuel tank, and said he'd see us in a couple of months. He was starting a tour across the USA. We were amazed that Herbie would undertake such an adventure while still recovering from his war wounds. We hoped he'd stay safe and looked forward to hearing about his travels.

After six weeks on the road, Herbie came back from his "Easy Rider" adventure. He'd traveled to New Orleans, up the Mississippi, through the Badlands, and returned to Southern California. He was happy to be home, and we were thrilled to see him. He had countless stories to tell.

I moved in with Herbie and Larry to a new adult apartment complex called "The Californian" in Santa Ana. These were nice units that had a weight room, jacuzzi, sauna, and a large swimming pool in the middle, perfect for parties. We found work with Bob Freeman Landscaping.

Drugs, sex, and rock and roll were common in our apartment. Larry's brother was a major drug dealer who showed up one day and gave Larry a whole kilo of marijuana. Paranoid about having that much pot around, Larry decided to make some money while smoking it. He asked me to help him divide it into small bags we called "lids." We locked ourselves in the bathroom and started breaking up the hard-packed marijuana, rolling joints, and smoking as we worked. Pot residue covered everything—us and every surface in the bathroom. The smell was overwhelming throughout the apartment. Gripped by paranoia, we spent the next two days scrubbing the place clean, using fifty cans of aerosol deodorant before we felt satisfied.

LSD occasionally showed up at the apartment. Hippie friends shared their acid stories with me. Although nervous about it, I decided to try it anyway. One night, we dropped a tab of "Purple Haze." It took a while to kick in. I didn't notice anything until I ran my fingers through the carpet fibers on the floor, where tiny people seemed to be traveling through the strands. A friend looked at me and asked in a strange, contorted, slow voice if I was high yet, his eyes as big as dinner plates. When Larry's girlfriend started talking to me, I couldn't understand a word she said. I had to get out of there.

Brian and I went outside, and I became convinced I was Nero, the Roman Emperor. I stood on a plant stand and delivered this incredible speech while Brian cheered below, clapping and spinning in tight circles. The trees and plants transformed into flat neon lights. I entered another world. As the night wore on, I found myself in our apartment bathroom, looking in the mirror. My face was covered in big, ugly warts. Was I really that hideous? I picked up a razor blade and held it to my throat, watching the hallucination of cutting my throat with blood and tissue gushing out. Terrified, I threw the razor blade in the toilet and cowered in the corner, desperately returning to normal.

This wasn't my last experience with LSD. When I asked a close friend who uses heavily why I had a bad trip, he said, "You didn't do enough. Double it up and you'll see what I mean."

My next LSD trip was at a Led Zeppelin concert at Olympic Stadium in Los Angeles. We went with a heavy drug user in his 1960 Chevy. We dropped a tab upon arrival and waited for it to kick in. The concert was incredible, starting with Quicksilver Messenger Service to cheers from three thousand people. They delivered an electrifying, otherworldly performance. We waited an hour for Led Zeppelin, completely zonked.

Led Zeppelin captured our souls—there was no escape. We danced as if there was no tomorrow.

When the concert ended, the three of us went back to the car, but our driver was nowhere to be found. We waited until first light, sitting on the curb, unsure of what to do. Deciding to get some food, we wandered the streets of LA, with LSD still flowing through our veins, staring at the tops of high-rises. Eventually, we found a restaurant run by the prison system for work-release inmates. Each inmate waiter looked like they could slit your throat without warning, but the coffee was excellent. After breakfast, we hitchhiked home, never finding out what happened to our driver.

After that experience, I decided to quit drugs entirely. They scared me and pushed me into deep depression.

Surfing Baja

We surfed Baja California back then. It wasn't crowded, and it felt like something out of Hemingway. Drinking beer in small seaside cantinas and stopping at different surf spots along the coast. We always ended up in San Miguel, just north of Ensenada.

When we heard about the great surf at Mazatlán and San Blas, Herbie, Rick, Larry, and I packed up Larry's Ford Econoline camper van. We loaded it with surfboards on top, rolled up the side awning, and took off. Crossing the border south of Yuma, we drove down the Mexican roads.

It didn't take long for us to get our first flat tire. After changing to the spare, we hit the road again. Mexican roads have plenty of tire shops, and we soon figured out why.

We stopped only for gas and beer. When one driver got tired, we switched. Then, at two in the morning, another flat tire occurred, and this time we didn't have a spare. Two of us hitched a ride for two hours to the next village. Surprisingly, we found a tire shop — a galvanized tin-sided building with a dirt floor, front wide open, and a cot in the back. The old man who ran it lived there and looked like he hadn't bathed in months, but he fixed our tire for a dollar and a half.

After three days of nonstop driving, we arrived at the northern outskirts of Mazatlán. Late in the afternoon, we headed straight for the water and found an open stretch of undeveloped beach. Just in front of us, there was a lovely peak breaking between two and three feet. Exhausted from the trip, we grabbed our boards and surfed these sweet waves until we couldn't see anymore. By flashlight, we rolled out our sleeping bags and slept under a sky full of stars.

At first light, the surf picked up to four or five feet. I went out again.

We found a campsite called Lupe's just north of Mazatlán. Noticing a hot left break off a rocky point, we checked in and set up camp. Perfect six-foot lefts were rolling in with nobody out. That was the most blissful surfing I can remember. Wave after wave to myself for over an hour.

After two days at Lupe's, we headed to San Blas. As we entered town, we drove through the jungle. Three of us climbed onto the van while Larry drove, making a grand entrance into the town center, which featured a typical Catholic cathedral and a well-maintained park with a fountain in the middle.

That's where we stopped and found two gringo surfers sitting on a concrete park bench.

"You should have been here yesterday!" they said.

The swell had gone down in the night, the same swell we'd caught at Lupe's.

"Still surfable waves over at Matachen Bay," they claimed.

After touring San Blas and grabbing a bite to eat, we headed to Matachen Bay—a beautiful, sizable bay. To get to the point, we drove along the north side of the beach for about a mile, watching waves peel off smoothly on a steady right shoulder. The surf was small but looked like it had potential for a fun ride.

The day we arrived, we met a group of people our age. They were hippies, not surfers. A cute girl was with them, probably between eighteen and twenty, wearing a sheer, see-through nightgown that barely covered her, with nothing underneath. She occasionally lifted her gown, revealing herself, but no one else seemed to notice. I noticed.

Bug bites covered her, and I quickly learned why. No-see-ums were tiny, nearly invisible flies that packed a punch when they bit. The only relief from these bugs was to go out in the water.

I paddled out and caught a wave that I rode for a mile. It was fun, but I wished it had been bigger. When the wave petered out, I walked a mile back to the point carrying my surfboard, harassed by no-see-ums all the way. I stayed in the water until late afternoon when a Mexican started a fire, burning coconut husks. Billowing white smoke rose from the fire, chasing away the no-see-ums. It was nice to get relief from those pesky flies, but then we had to deal with the smoke.

The rest of the evening was spent talking with our new friends. The nearly naked young girl kept scratching herself.

In the morning, the surf eased up, so we packed our gear and headed home. We wanted to share our great experience with our friends. After three days and five flat tires, we crossed the border at Yuma, finally back in familiar territory.

Once I returned from Mexico, I began experiencing episodes of severe depression. I didn't realize at the time, but I was dealing with post-traumatic stress from the war.

I used my GI Bill benefits to go to college. It only lasted a couple of months. Listening to my professors, I got madder than hell. I never knew what triggered me. I hung out with Rick Usher, a good-looking guy who delivered flowers for a living. During our free time, we went body surfing at 17th Street in Newport Beach. We discussed the importance of having a dark tan for boosting self-esteem. He thought I wasn't quite right, but neither of us could figure out why.

It was about that time that my DT-1 got stolen. I was back hitchhiking.

Dad was starting a new house down in Carlsbad. I quit my job with Bob Freeman Landscaping and went to work for him, thinking a change might do me good. That lasted two weeks. Hitchhiking home, I was picked up by Bill Lyman in a brand-new station wagon. He was the co-owner of Lyman and Woods Construction. They had a contract with the City of San Diego to lay sewer pipes for a major land development project.

During our conversation, I mentioned that I had recently left the Marines as a heavy equipment operator. He asked if I wanted a job laying sewer pipes. The job paid $6.50 an hour—big money at the time—plus hotel room and food money. I took it.

The work wasn't difficult. A ditch digger carved out a trench four feet wide and ten feet deep. We established a grade at the bottom of the trench. The crane lowered a section of sewer pipe, and we connected the 3' x 20' pipe using a rubber gasket. After backfilling the trench and compacting the soil, we laid asphalt over the top.

I did what I was told and got along with the other workers. I was making a lot of money.

Two of the guys I worked with were hillbilly types who operated a backhoe, and I enjoyed working with them. One of them had a 1959 yellow Ford pickup with a camper shell on the back. The pickup was in excellent shape. He wanted to buy a new Ford Courier pickup and asked if I wanted to buy his truck for $500. I bought it.

On weekends, I drove back to our apartment and went surfing at 17th Street with Rick Usher, Herbie, and Larry.

Herbie was using more drugs, drinking, and struggling to keep a job.

Conversion

Lighthouse Ranch - Table Bluff, California

Even though I was making good money, had my truck, and surf buddies I enjoyed hanging out with, I couldn't shake this depression.

Rick Usher arrived at my apartment in a cheerful and lively mood. The first thing I noticed was that he wasn't cursing. Phrases like "Praise God," "Thank you, Jesus," and "Hallelujah" flowed from his mouth. This was not Rick I knew. I asked him what was going on.

He responded joyously, "I found Jesus!"

My grandparents took me to church when I was in my early teens, but I never took it seriously. When my grandmother let me go to Sunday school, I skipped it and went to the gas station on the corner to smoke cigarettes. I wasn't completely unaware of religion, but it was right in front of me through a friend I admired. I listened to Rick share his experience. He invited me to a meeting that night at Calvary Chapel, a small church in Tustin. It was crowded with young people carrying the cross of Christ. Since Rick was such a good friend, I decided to go.

The meeting started at 7 o'clock. I was amazed by the number of young people. They were diverse in appearance, representing counterculture types with long hair and beards, as well as so-called straight people. There were more people outside the church than inside. Oversized sliding glass doors opened, with people standing twenty or thirty deep. Inside was standing room only. **Love Song**, a Christian rock group, played fantastic music! Hands were raised skyward, with one finger in the air.

People swayed to the music. This hippie guy named Lonnie Frisbee started preaching the gospel.

When he finished, he asked for a show of hands from those wanting to know Jesus. Uncontrollably, I raised my hand and moved forward with the others. Lonnie prayed for each person. He came to me and touched me. I was zonked. I was now part of the "Jesus People."

It later became known that Lonnie Frisbee was a closeted gay man. They asked him to step down. He later died of AIDS.

I heard about a Christian outreach house in Northern California where some of my friends had moved. When I visited, they told me about a Christian commune started by Ken Smith at the Lighthouse on Table Bluff.

I drove to the Lighthouse and met Ken Smith. The scene was stunning: a group of white concrete buildings, a lighthouse perched on the cliff overlooking the Pacific Ocean, and a tall, white water tower. It was the Table Bluff Coast Guard Station, built years earlier as part of the coastal defenses during the war. The entire area was called the Lighthouse Ranch.

Back in San Diego, I quit my job with Lyman and Woods Construction, loaded up my pickup with a few belongings, and moved to the Lighthouse Ranch.

Living at the ranch was blissful. I didn't do much besides sing gospel songs, read the Bible, and pray. Ken believed in living by faith. Living by faith, we prayed and waited for some local churches to bring food and money to keep things afloat. I wasn't eating well. The food we did get, the sisters prepared in the makeshift kitchen. The dining room had long tables and benches, in what was the old workshop in the main building. Sometimes we watched our food go cold as we prayed for an hour. It didn't really matter how cold our food was—our souls were being cleansed.

Word spread among travelers, and more people stopped by to visit. Soon, three hundred people lived at the ranch.

Makeshift living setups were spread across the property, including vans, old cars, lean-tos, and tents. Some slept directly on the ground. The only requirement to stay was attending the morning prayer meetings, which ended with a gospel message.

On Sunday mornings, we loaded into whatever transportation was available and headed into Eureka for church service. The only church in town that accepted these smelly hippies was a small church called Deliverance Temple. At DT, as it was known, the lead pastor was a former preacher from the Assembly of God named Jim Durkin. Jim looked more like a used car salesman than a preacher. He was overweight, with a round, ruddy, pockmarked face, dressed in cheap suits and wearing a wide tie. He had a heart for these smelly hippies. On the side, he and his Oklahoma-born wife, Dacie, ran a real estate business.

Jim wasn't much to look at, but he sure could preach.

DT was a Pentecostal Church known for speaking in tongues and dancing in the Spirit. Before the hippies arrived, Jim had a congregation of twelve elderly members. The people of Lighthouse Ranch were warmly welcomed.

Jim started an outreach house for travelers on the corner of Clark and B Streets, called "Clark and B." Larry Johnson, fresh from Haight-Ashbury in San Francisco, ran the place. The local police supported it because it provided them with a place to send vagrants.

With a shared vision, Ken and Jim began working closely together. Jim visited the ranch and held weekly Bible studies, giving Ken many chances to preach at the Sunday church service. A diverse group of colorful people gathered at the ranch.

Leon Umveg, before converting, used to drop three hundred tabs of LSD at a time. He was off his rocker. Leon changed his name to David, after King David in the Bible. This steely-eyed lunatic with a long beard quoted scripture from memory in King James English. He believed we should speak in King James English because it was closer to the original language. Some tried to tell him that the original Bible languages were Greek, Hebrew, and Aramaic, but he was unmoved.

David died of a massive heart attack while sitting at a bus stop, clutching his King James Bible. I'm sure he was welcomed to the beyond.

With young sisters at the ranch, fresh from the streets of free love and sex, Ken fell to his temptations. It wasn't hard for Ken to take advantage; they idolized him. He'd had this problem before. It was the reason he moved to Eureka after being ostracized by the Church in Oregon.

With Ken's credibility damaged, Jim and DT offered to buy the ranch and take control of the ministry. Ken agreed and moved back to Oregon to build houses. DT, the Lighthouse Ranch, and Clark and B merged to create Gospel Outreach (GO).

The difference between Ken and Jim was that Jim believed hippies should work and support themselves. That realization emptied half the population at the Ranch.

The first business Jim started was selling junk jewelry door-to-door. More businesses followed later. With a big male crew, we teamed up with a company that salvages train wrecks. They rented large trucks and took us to the train wreck site, where we camped along the tracks and loaded as many boxcars as possible onto flatbed trucks. There was a time limit on how long we could work before the insurance company covered the remaining wreckage. No one received payment; the money went to the ministry.

We received tree planting contracts across Northern California, Oregon, and Washington State. We replanted clear-cut timberland in remote backwoods areas during heavy rain. Before it was over, we had established a variety of services, including carpet cleaning, vinyl repair, lawn maintenance, fire restoration, pottery, and a daily newspaper for advertisers. The money went to the ministry.

I Get Married

I met Lucille during a visit to Calvary Chapel in Costa Mesa. She was engaged to the violin player with the Christian rock group, **Love Song**. Without asking, a caring Christian friend borrowed my yellow truck and totaled it. It was God's will. As a result, I hitchhiked down from Eureka to Orange County, a tough three-day journey. Many nights, I was stranded on some obscure on-ramp at two in the morning, freezing my ass off.

On this occasion, I traveled with a friend, a convert at the Lighthouse who worked at an organic garden in Hydesville, a small-town east of Fortuna. He was from Tustin and went to school with Lucille, who was eighteen. She was a member of Calvary Chapel. I was introduced to her there.

Lucille invited us to her family's house the next day, where we met her mother, who was an actor's agent. Her mother had secured contracts for Lucille and her brothers to appear in TV commercials. Lucille was excited about a future career in modeling and acting. Her father worked as a meat cutter at Safeway Markets.

We told Lucille about the ranch and encouraged her to come for the summer to grow in the Lord. That summer, lovely Lucille went to the ranch. She was pretty, well-endowed, and my friend secretly hoped to marry her. The two of them prayed and decided they were not to be. Besides, she was engaged to the violin player.

I was horny all the time, but at the ranch, we could only enjoy sex if we were married—except if you were Ken Smith. I set my sights on Lucille. One thing led to another. We got married in the former workshop, now the dining room, in the big white building. David (Leon Umveg) gazed up to heaven, raised his hands, and praised the Lord. It wasn't much of a ceremony, but we were free to indulge.

Our honeymoon involved packing some camping gear and catching a ride thirty miles inland, where we found a spot on the Mad River. We camped there for three days. One night, a mountain lion came down to the river for a drink and didn't eat us. We hitchhiked back to the ranch on a lumber truck.

When it was time to tell her parents, the news didn't go over very well. We were of age, and there was nothing they could do about it. Plus, it was the will of God. The violin player was a bit jaded.

We lived in a room above the kitchen called the married couples' dorm. It was nicer than the other living spaces and included a communal bathroom and shower.

Lucille and I were part of the train wreck team, traveling in large trucks to the salvage sites and setting up camp. I was one of the drivers, and she sat up front with me. For us, this was exciting work and a true adventure, and we felt good knowing we were supporting the others in Gospel Outreach.

It didn't take long for Lucille to become pregnant. We felt a deep sense of pride as her belly began to grow, and we looked forward to having a child, a true blessing from God. Everything seemed to go well until the seventh month when her water broke, and we rushed to the hospital in Fortuna. After thirty-six hours of intense labor, the baby boy was born. He lived for about thirty minutes. The medical team did all they could, but it wasn't enough.

It was a heartbreaking time. In the recovery room, I sat next to Lucille, crying uncontrollably. She reached over and took my hand, telling me it would be okay.

I kept crying.

The Ministry Grows

People continued to arrive, and numerous conversions were taking place. The ministry was evolving. Jim and Dacie owned several old houses across the area that they wanted to rent out. Married couples and a few other people were supposed to move from the ranch into these houses. Lucille and I moved to the Elk River Roadhouse with two other couples. We had daily devotions and took part in outreach activities and church services.

One fall, a large group of us traveled up to apple country in Northern Washington State to pick apples. We could eat as many apples as we wanted, but we had to pick each apple off the tree before we got paid. Apple farms were set up to host groups like ours. They provided dorms, big kitchens, mess halls, and a fun experience for most. The apples were so crisp and juicy that we couldn't get enough.

The next year, we harvested grapes for big wineries because it was closer to home.

Two hippie communes fully converted to Christianity. One was Gopher Ville, west of Garberville, California. Gopher Ville was founded by Tony, whose parents were wealthy from San Francisco. Tony never had to work. He bought the land to try to bring people together after he jumped off a dam during an LSD trip. He received this vision for Gopher Ville during his recovery. After the hippie conversions, they had baptisms in the nude. Tony and his wife Jane became two of the prominent leaders in Gospel Outreach.

Another commune was Sabina's Land on Navarro Ridge in Mendocino. Sabina, originally from Germany, was a remarkable person—beautiful beyond words. She survived the Dresden bombings during World War II and later moved to Washington, DC. She married into the Ball family, and her husband was a close friend of Richard Nixon. Sabina started using LSD, divorced her husband, and moved west. When she and her commune converted to Christianity, she came to Eureka seeking guidance from Gospel Outreach on what to do next. Sabina's Land changed into The Lord's Land, and Lucille and I were sent to help.

The priority was to settle multiple marriages. Several men found jobs at a large mobile home park being built on Compche Road. It was enjoyable to dive for abalone off the coast, and there was a large organic garden. Several potters living on the land started Maranatha Pottery Works. They sold their products throughout the Northwest. The earnings supported the commune—a legitimate form of Christian communism.

A colorful character on Navarro Ridge was Jim Sansee. Jim was tall and thin, always wearing a smile. His blue overalls were short in the legs, ending above his high-top leather boots. He'd lived there forever. Jim ran a small, one-owner sawmill. He sawed up timber for us to use on our many projects around the property. News came that Jim had a terrible accident and died. Asked what happened, the tale was gruesome. Pieces of Jim's clothing got caught on the track and dragged him through the saw blade, cutting him in half. We had to find an alternative location to obtain our lumber.

We were taking our turn at tree planting when disaster struck. The truck delivering our crew crashed into a tree, killing three of our members. Receiving the devastating phone call at two in the morning, I rushed to the hospital at Fort Bragg to be with the survivors. How could this happen? Shortly afterward, Lucille and I returned to Eureka.

Sabina later passed away after returning to Germany to work with troubled youth. Tony collapsed in his neighbor's kitchen from a massive heart attack while in the early stages of Alzheimer's. God was merciful.

Lucille and I moved out of the commune and rented our own apartment. It wasn't much—an old house divided into three separate apartments. Still an essential part of the ministry, I became involved in the leadership team that set ministry policy.

Gospel Outreach was recognized as part of a national movement in Christian ministries. Loose affiliations started forming with like-minded counterculture groups as they experienced a spontaneous Christian revival.

Lucille and I struggled with the loss of our son but did our best to carry on. God's grace helped us get through it. While dealing with my ongoing depression and grief, I started doing remodeling work with a man named Dwight Nash. Dwight and his wife, Evelyn, were older but liked what they saw at DT and became members.

We Go to Alaska

Dwight and Evelyn had come from Alaska, where their son, also named Dwight, lived and worked for the phone company. They owned a dairy farm in the Mendenhall Valley, located below the Mendenhall Glacier, ten miles north of Juneau. News of what was happening in the lower forty-eight reached Alaska. Dwight Jr. (DJ) belonged to a house church group that wanted to reach out to local youth. Dwight Senior asked Lucille and me to consider traveling to Alaska to work with his son and set up an outreach house. It didn't take us long to decide, as we thought the change would be good for us. A week later, we were on our way through Canada to Prince Rupert in a van full of construction materials. We caught the ferry to Juneau. Dwight Senior was going to remodel DJ's house, dig out a basement, and I was planning to help.

Driving through British Columbia was incredibly beautiful in the middle of summer. The temperature was in the nineties. Our route took us along Highway 1 to Hope, then 97 to Prince George, where we turned west onto the Yellowhead Highway.

Prince Rupert, a sizable city known for its fishing industry, was the first stop for the Alaska State Ferry, which took us to Juneau. We arrived just in time to load our van onto the ferry, which resembled a cruise ship.

Aboard, we slept in the main salon on plush reclining chairs. There were three restaurants on board, as well as numerous glass observation areas, as we traveled through the inland waterway.

The ferry stopped at various villages along the way, unloading and loading passengers. The first stop was Ketchikan, then Wrangell and Petersburg, before we reached Juneau. The trip lasted three days. It was hard to believe how beautiful the place was. If asked what the most beautiful spot on Earth is, I'd say Alaska.

From the ferry, we saw humpback whales totally breach out of the water, sometimes two in unison. We observed a pod of killer whales attacking a lone humpback. Open-mouthed, the killer whales tore long strips of flesh off the poor humpback's flank.

DJ, his son, and his wife, Hildegard, greeted us upon our arrival. Hildegard was from Germany. They met while DJ was serving in the Army. DJ was a quiet type, and Hildegard was even more tranquil.

Living on the shore of Auke Bay, their house was situated on a sloping waterfront lot with a breathtaking view of Coghlan Island across a wide channel. Pods of porpoises and killer whales played along the shoreline. Fishing was top-notch—salmon and halibut were the primary catches.

With these surroundings, it was hard to focus on a youth outreach program. There was just so much else to enjoy. In the first couple of days, DJ and Hilde took us to see the local sights. We visited the Mendenhall Glacier and the end of the road where Berners Bay lay.

Berners Bay was perfectly calm that day, with towering snow-capped mountains reflected in the glassy water. Colors blazed across open fields of multi-colored wildflowers, beckoning one to run through them barefoot, surrounded by spectacular scenery to feast one's eyes upon.

Dwight Senior was eager to start on the basement and wasted no time excavating under the house by hand and wheelbarrow. He braced it up, hoping it wouldn't collapse on us. On weekends, we gathered in a small house group that they called church. Six couples prayed and sang a few songs. Then Dave, the house group leader, delivered a gospel message.

Dave had an old Owens cabin cruiser that he'd set up for commercial fishing. When he wasn't working for the phone company, he and his wife were out fishing. I was invited the following weekend, accepted, and couldn't wait to hook into a big king salmon.

Fishing in Alaska isn't like fishing anywhere else. The summer sun didn't set. DJ had a small runabout. We could quit at five or six, have a quick meal, jump in the boat, and troll for salmon until ten or eleven at night. On weekends, I went out with Dave much farther, made a little money, and ate plenty of salmon.

On one trip, we saw a large flock of seagulls on the water's surface. Dave mentioned they were likely waiting for a school of baitfish to rise. We headed toward the birds, hoping to hook up. As we approached, less than twenty feet off our port side, a humpback whale breached out of the water.

The whale and I were eye to eye, with tons of water and krill spilling from its wide-open mouth. The boat rocked wildly as we fought to keep our balance. We watched the frothy water left behind in its trail.

Halibut fishing was my favorite activity. When fishing for halibut, you knew to look for a halibut hole where the big ones rested. Dave had local knowledge of these spots. He would bait a large hook with heavy fishing line and lower it to the bottom. Usually, halibut ranged from 25 to 400 pounds, but the best-tasting ones were in the 25-to-40-pound range.

They also had a tough time getting into the boat. Larger ones had to be killed first before they could be pulled in. Those were nothing but slabs of muscle—if not killed beforehand, they would tear up the boat. The usual way to kill a large fish was to shoot it in the head with a .38 pistol. Halibut had to be gaffed between the two gills just under the mouth. Realizing its fate, it went berserk, flailing and smashing against the side of the boat.

I gaffed a 60-pound fish. It was all I could do to hold on. I got soaked from the flying water, panicked, and yelled at Dave to shoot it. The first two shots missed; the third shot did the job. And that was only a sixty-pound fish. I couldn't imagine what a 300-pounder would be like.

Old-time Alaskans are called sourdoughs. One elderly sourdough lived just a few houses down from DJ, on another beautiful piece of land facing the bay. With his boat docked in front of his home, his favorite hobby was fishing for halibut. Well into his seventies, he had a girlfriend in her twenties.

She wasn't much to look at, but she kept him warm through cold winter nights.

His family traveled from the lower forty-eight to visit him. They planned to go halibut fishing. With his family on the boat, he realized he'd left his pistol on top of the fireplace mantel.

Hurrying back, he grabbed the pistol and let it fall onto the brick hearth. After waiting a moment, a member of the group went to see what was delaying the old sourdough. He found the old man lying on the floor, dead in a pool of blood. The gun had gone off when it hit the bricks, shooting him in the heart.

Summer turned to fall, and duck and goose hunting season opened. One young man in the house group, an avid bird hunter, invited me to join him. Borrowing one of his many shotguns, we dressed in our hunting gear and waded into a marshy estuary. As the temperature started to drop, snow lines crept down the surrounding mountains. A flock of Canada geese flew within range, and we fired our shotguns. He got two. I missed.

I can't say I enjoyed bird hunting much, but I went out several times hoping it would grow on me. I bought a used single-shot shotgun. After a while, it sat in the closet.

Winter was approaching. The days became shorter and colder. The basement project was progressing well. We excavated what we needed, poured a concrete slab for the floor, and framed the walls. The house was now secure, with no risk of collapse.

Dwight Senior traveled down to the lower forty-eight to handle business. There were three feet of snow on the ground, and it was light for a few hours during the day. The situation with the house group was becoming uncertain. Nobody knew what to do or how to accomplish it. I suggested we start an outreach house in Juneau, but that idea wasn't well-received. Our relationship with the house group was falling apart.

I got a job making donuts at the American Bakery, owned by John and Ann Linbeck. Lucille and I rented a trailer across the bridge, on the outskirts of Douglas, right off the road. John and Ann, recently converted, lived down the road, and Lucille and Ann became good friends. I enjoyed making donuts, and the bakery was always warm inside. Naturally, I started gaining a few pounds from eating the scraps.

John's weakness was a terrible temper. If things didn't go smoothly in the bakery, he threw whatever he could reach across the room. Many days, I ducked to avoid flying pots, pans, trays, or utensils. What scared me most was the lids of one-gallon tin cans. One of those lids could cut your jugular.

They began experiencing marriage problems. Ann fell in love with an older writer. They soon separated. John sold the bakery and moved to Seattle. I never heard from him again. Ann married the older writer.

Dave and I were fishing in Barlow Cove on the northern end of Admiralty Island when a small float plane landed and motored up to us. The pilot, standing on the float, asked if we had heard anything. We told him no, nothing. When we asked what happened, he said there had been a plane crash. What he didn't tell us was that an Alaska Airlines 737 had crashed into a mountain, killing everyone on board. Back in Juneau, everybody knew someone on that flight. Many lost loved ones. It took months for the community to recover from the tragedy.

Lucille and I gravitated toward people living in Juneau. We started associating with the Assembly of God Church, trying to keep a youth outreach program alive. That was the reason we came to Alaska in the first place.

I went to work building luxury homes with Elmer Ignell, a contractor who was a member of the church. Winter wasn't easy—we framed the buildings in terrible weather. Construction in Alaska: if you weren't willing to work in the harshest weather conditions, you didn't work. Eventually, you got used to it.

Elmer and Ramona, his wife, had a beautiful and talented daughter. She led the youth group at her church and was the choir's director. She had a lovely voice and sang many solos. To further her career, she left for Bible college in Montana. During an outing with other students, she was driving a van, went off the road, and hit a tree, killing her instantly. It was a terrible loss that devastated the entire community.

Lucille's brother came to experience Alaska, and I arranged a job for him with Elmer. He loved the wilderness. He made a friend, and they would often go canoe camping in remote areas on weekends. One weekend, it nearly cost them their lives. While canoeing in open water, a fierce storm suddenly arose. It was a close call for a while, with the canoe nearly swamped. If it had happened, he and his friend would have been just another statistic. One didn't last long in the cold Alaskan waters.

We opened an outreach house in downtown Juneau with help from the local church. A couple traveled up from Eureka with another friend, Steve, to assist with the outreach. Steve lived in the basement of the house. He tried to involve local youth from the church, but unfortunately, none showed interest. He ended up taking care of drunk Indians, ex-cons, and lunatics. It wasn't what the local people envisioned, but coming from the Lighthouse Ranch, we were used to it.

One lunatic was truly crazy. Someone asked what time it was, and the next day, twenty alarm clocks were scattered throughout the house. The ticking drove us insane. We couldn't figure out where all the clocks were coming from. Something similar happened with oranges. Someone said they loved oranges, and the next day, hundreds appeared. We realized what was going on when a vendor from a local store tried to deposit a check for the clocks, but the signature didn't match. He had stolen one of our checkbooks and was cashing bad checks. We finally got rid of him after he kept dropping his pants at one of our meetings and exposing himself to children.

An ex-con was once a gourmet chef. He took over the kitchen and prepared fantastic, elaborate meals that were well beyond our budget. When I asked him to scale back the meals, he lost his temper, smashing everything in sight. He was asked to leave.

Angoon

I met Peter Jack, the Tlingit Indian chief from Angoon, a small village on the west side of Admiralty Island. We got along well, and he invited me to visit his village.

There were two ways to reach Angoon: by boat or by seaplane. We opted for the plane. Flying in Alaska was always unpredictable. Sometimes you made it, and sometimes you didn't. The weather could change in just minutes. Southeast Alaska was usually overcast or rainy.

The plane that flew to Angoon was an old, well-taped-together Grumman Goose, a WWII-era seaplane. I was looking forward to my first experience on a seaplane. We gathered at the marina's mooring area in town. The pilot informed us that the weather conditions were marginal, but he was proceeding anyway.

Strapped in, the pilot started the engine and taxied out to the main channel. Once he saw no boats in the way, he gunned the engine. Gaining speed, water splashed up each side of the plane.

Once airborne, there was no turning back, or so I thought.

Aloft, the plane turned right, passing over Douglas Island and crossing Stephens Passage. Admiralty Island was ahead, and the ceiling was lowering. The pilot had to hurry to get across the island before the clouds dropped any further, or we'd be in deep trouble. He thought he could make it and reach the other side of the island in time.

We didn't make it. The ceiling dropped like a rock as we flew nestled in a not-so-wide valley. Turning back, the pilot sharply banked the plane, and I felt my eyeballs about to explode. He must have been pulling three Gs. With that much pressure on this old, taped-together Grumman Goose, I was convinced it was going to fall apart. We had only a few hundred yards to complete the turn—and we could have crashed into the side of a mountain. After finishing the turn, we flew over the tree-studded island and saw the water again, a welcome sight. Home safe.

The next day, we tried again. The Grumman Goose landed in Favorite Bay and taxied to the seaplane dock. Peter Jack was there to meet us. He took us to his house, where his wife and other village women prepared a small meal for us.

The main course was fried bread. They mixed up a batter similar to donut mix, deep-fried it in hot oil, and sprinkled it with sugar. Looking around at the ladies, we could tell this was one of their favorite meals.

The church elders organized a meeting for us to discuss establishing an outreach house. They were worried about the alcohol problem that was common in their tribes. They asked for any help they could get. The entire village was there—standing room only—in their small church.

That evening, I enjoyed a venison dinner at Peter Jack's house. I wanted to learn more about what life was like in an isolated Tlingit village, but it wasn't easy. Tlingits don't say much, and when they do, it's hard to tell if they're genuinely interested in what they tell you. They speak in a low monotone with an expressionless, blank look on their faces.

I learned that Peter Jack was a licensed hunting guide. Hunters from the lower forty-eight booked trips with him. I saw hunters land at Juneau Airport, dressed in the latest L.L. Bean gear, carrying a couple of hunting rifles in bags, and wearing $500 hunting boots. They flew to Angoon, and Peter Jack would meet them and set them up in a small hunting lodge. In the morning, dressed in a dirty T-shirt, polyester pants, and loafers, he served them a hearty breakfast. After breakfast, they walked out on a trail about 200 yards from the lodge. With his handmade deer call, he called for a few bucks. Hunters would shoot their buck, bag it, and head back to the lodge in around 30 minutes. At the lodge, he dressed the bucks and sent the hunters on their way to create stories of their great Alaskan adventure.

He owned and captained a fifty-foot purse seine fishing boat, the livelihood that sustained the village. During fishing season, he took his boat out along with many others to search for schools of salmon. When they found a school, the tender set the net by circling it and then brought the end back to the big boat. The crew winched in the net, making a large purse around the fish and hauling them aboard. He said they had good years and bad ones. Hopefully, the good years made up for the bad.

The competition between boats and crews during the short salmon season is fierce. Peter Jack had recently regained his fishing license from the fisheries department. He hadn't fished in two years due to a run-in with another boat and captain.

His license had been suspended while the investigation was ongoing. He was hit by another boat, which led to a violent confrontation between the two captains.

Corking happens when one fishing boat is positioned over a school of fish to set its nets. Another boat tries to fish inside the first boat's area and steal its fish. This time, he was corked but didn't want trouble, so he let the other boat take the fish. Problems arose when their nets got tangled. He asked the other captain to move his boat so he could retrieve his net. They refused, and Peter nudged the other boat out of the way.

The other captain went ballistic and drew weapons. Peter cleared his net and fished for the rest of the day. When returning to port, fishery officials met him and impounded his boat. The other boat had filed a formal complaint, claiming that Peter had rammed it. They placed a patch over the spot where Peter's boat hit them. Peter said there was no damage to the other boat during the encounter.

After a two-year investigation, it was found that the other boat had applied the patch on the wrong side. Peter Jack was cleared, but he lost two years of fishing.

An Alaskan Baby is on the Way

The news took our breath away. We got another chance! Our second Alaska winter was starting when we received the life-changing call.

"You're pregnant!" the doctor exclaimed.

Having lost our first baby, we wanted to ensure we did everything right this time. Lucille chose natural childbirth and began attending classes at the local hospital, while I focused on being her coach. Local women went out of their way to meet our needs. The outpouring of support was remarkable, especially considering the distance from home.

Our neighbors in Douglas were a friendly, older couple who welcomed us warmly. The wife was happy to have young people next door and especially excited about Lucille having a baby. She did everything she could to help us. They kept two VW Bugs under a carport by the road. Dave's mobile home, where we were living, was just twenty feet from that carport.

The Crash

The heater was enough to keep us warm during the cold winter, allowing us to sleep comfortably without needing clothing. At two in the morning on a freezing night when Lucille was six months pregnant, there was a terrible crash. Our mobile home blew up.

We were pushed through a thin plywood bulkhead into the next room. Electricity crackled all around the wreckage. We could hardly breathe as dust filled our mouths and nostrils. We had no idea what had happened. A loud, irritating, hissing noise filled the air.

The woman next door was yelling, "THEY'RE DEAD! THEY'RE DEAD! THOSE POOR KIDS ARE DEAD!"

Regaining my senses, I realized a car had crashed into what used to be our kitchen. People were already gathering to help.

One man yelled, "IS THERE ANYBODY IN THERE?"

"Yes! Don't come in—we don't have any clothes on!"

We scrambled desperately through the rubble to find something to wear. Someone was stuck in the car. The annoying hissing noise was the broken radiator, hot water boiling out.

I saw a face in the car and asked, "Are you okay?"

A voice replied weakly, "I don't know. Can you get me out of here?"

People rushed through the wreckage to reach us. One man pried open the back door, lifted Lucille, and carried her to the neighbor's house. The woman next door was so upset that she was shaking badly and crying as she wrapped Lucille in a blanket and held her close. In disbelief, I tried to make sense of what had happened.

I was amazed at how quickly the fire trucks and ambulance arrived. The paramedics rushed into the house and gave us a quick examination, ensuring we were stable enough to be moved. The word "miscarriage" came up, and I started to worry. They took us to the emergency room with sirens blaring and lights flashing. The hospital staff was extremely kind as they performed a thorough examination, with worried expressions on their faces.

News spread quickly. Our friends gathered at the hospital to see if they could help. After a short stay, Elmer and Ramona Ignell offered their home for our recovery. Sitting in their living room and discussing what had happened, I started to feel a strange sensation—I was going into shock. Elmer recognized what was happening and lay me down with my feet elevated, talking me through it. I don't know what I would have done without him. As I slowly regained my composure, they showed us to their guest room. After a shower, we tried to sleep but couldn't. The scene kept replaying in our minds.

The next morning, Ramona prepared an excellent breakfast. Elmer drove me in his pickup truck to see if anything could be salvaged. The scene was heartbreaking. Our rented mobile home was shattered in half. The Chevy station wagon had already been taken away.

With help from the neighbors, we pieced together what had happened.

The young man driving had been drunk and was traveling far too fast on the icy road. He lost control while rounding the turn and hit a snowbank that launched him into the air. He struck the top of the carport, flying over the two VW Bugs inside (you could still see the tire marks on top of the cars), then crashed nose-first into our mobile home. It was a miracle that none of us were killed. He was bruised and cut up but had no serious injuries. While recovering in the hospital, he was arrested for drunk driving.

The case went to court a few months later. With a good lawyer, he was acquitted after convincing the jury that it was a malfunction in his Chevy station wagon.

A New Home

The road engineer with the state contract to maintain sixty miles of road around Juneau came to the Ignells' home. He offered a cabin outside of Juneau if we needed it and wouldn't charge rent until we got back on our feet.

More than grateful, we accepted his generous offer. The lovely two-bedroom house was set back off the road. Our friends helped us furnish it with odds and ends, and we moved in. Right across the road was prime bird-hunting territory. I was still trying to master duck hunting.

One of the men staying at the outreach house had an eight-year-old daughter he couldn't care for. He asked Lucille and me if she could stay with us until he got himself together. The young girl moved in and took over the second bedroom. She was very sweet and a pleasure to have around, doing dishes without being asked and keeping her room spotless.

One morning, I took out the trash and looked toward a grassy meadow. A black bear was sitting on its haunches, staring at me. I'd been told that black bears weren't as dangerous as brown bears, but they could be unpredictable. It made me nervous, but I soon forgot about it. A couple of days later, coffee cup in hand, I looked out the front window. A bear was sleeping on our front porch. I went to the closet and loaded my shotgun.

I'd heard that throwing firecrackers at bears would scare them away. I didn't want to shoot because a wounded bear is extremely dangerous. The commotion I caused in the cabin disturbed the bear, and it sauntered toward the back. Gun ready, I went out the front door and quietly moved to the side yard. Twenty-five yards away, the bear sat, looking at me. I figured if I fired a few rounds to his right, it would sound like firecrackers, and he would run off. He did run, but not very far.

Realizing I needed help, I called Fish and Game and explained our problem. An hour later, a ranger arrived towing a trailer with a ten-foot by three-foot galvanized pipe bear trap. One end had a metal grate, and the other had a trap door. I greeted the ranger and pointed him to the back of the house to set up the trap. That's when I got in trouble—he saw the spot where I'd been burning our trash. I got a lecture about how burning trash attracts bears. I apologized and promised never to burn trash again.

Setting the trap was simple. You open the trap door and attach it to a lever connected to a line that extends to the far end. There, you tie a burlap bag of herring to the line and wait. The ranger told us to call when we caught the bear.

I cleaned up the burn area and went inside. We took turns staying up and watching out the window, wondering if the bear would show up. Around eleven o'clock, he appeared. He saw the trap and approached it cautiously, moving slowly and sniffing up and down. He came to the baited end and tried to get his paw in, but it was too big. He circled around to the open end, stuck his head in, sniffed, and pulled back out, looking around. Then he climbed in halfway, lost his nerve, and came back out. He sat there with his nose in the air, gathering courage. Finally, he climbed in, scrunching on his belly. When he grabbed the bag of fish, he sprung the trap. We had him!

After waiting a little, we went outside to see our catch. The bear lay there quietly, not making a sound or struggling, as if he'd been through this before. We watched as he looked back at us with big, sad eyes.

I called the ranger, who immediately arrived to capture the bear. They sedated him and flew him to a wilderness area to release him. We never saw that bear again.

Tiger Olsen, the Old Sourdough

Tiger Olsen was a legend. He had killed a man in Montana back in the early twenties and escaped to Taku Inlet. For the rest of his life, he lived alone, surviving off the land—hunting, fishing, and growing potatoes in the summer. People would visit his homestead, bringing him necessities while listening to his tales of survival in the harsh climate.

Whenever he visited town, a crowd would gather and follow him everywhere. Some of the older women made sure he was well cared for.

I ran into him in downtown Juneau. Even in his late seventies, he was tall, well-built, and stood straight, with a handsome, weathered face. Beneath that tough exterior was a lonely man.

He was in town because of chest pains and needed to see a doctor. He didn't worry about the bill—someone always paid it. He was sent to the hospital for observation, and it just so happened that our first son was born while Tiger Olsen was there.

Jamie's Birth

Lucille's water broke, and the contractions started in earnest. Although we had planned a natural birth in our cabin, our friends and neighbors wouldn't hear of it. They insisted we go to the hospital, and it's good they did.

In the hospital, we practiced our natural childbirth techniques as planned, with me as her coach. The nurse checked on us periodically. It was a difficult labor. Contractions intensified as I watched her breathing and helped keep her relaxed. When she hyperventilated, we had a paper bag ready. This was going to be a big baby. It wouldn't be easy.

Hours passed as her contractions persisted. The nurse offered pain relief, but Lucille refused. We grew tired, hoping the baby would arrive soon. Lucille became so exhausted that she fell asleep between contractions, making it seem like one long ordeal. She was determined to give birth to this baby naturally. After many hours, the nurse said she was dilated to nine centimeters. It was time to move to the delivery room and bring in the doctor.

As her coach, I was permitted to be there while the nurse prepared the necessary instruments. The doctor arrived, examined her, and told her it was time to push.

Childbirth isn't pretty. Lucille pushed so hard her skin turned white and blotchy. The veins in her neck looked ready to burst. Her hair and face dripped with sweat, her face red as a beet, but none of that mattered now. That baby had to come out.

Despite our objections, the doctor administered an epidural, explaining that the baby was too large. The nurse pushed on Lucille's stomach with all her might, but the baby still held tight. I began to wonder if this struggle would ever come to an end.

Finally, the head emerged. The doctor turned the shoulders and out came our baby boy with blood splattering on the floor. Then blood began flowing from her uterus—lots of blood. She was hemorrhaging badly. The doctor shouted orders to the nurse, who became all business. Still more blood came.

The doctor pressed hard on Lucille's stomach while the nurse administered medications into her veins. Lucille became incoherent and trembled uncontrollably. I was instructed to leave the room. This blissful moment was frightening.

Outside, I heard the commotion. Our baby cried for the first time. In the waiting room, I sat down, exhausted and worried. After what felt like an eternity, the doctor came in and assured me everything was fine. Lucille was stabilized, and I was able to see her.

In the recovery room, she lay cleaned up as if nothing had happened, lying on her side and dozing with our baby boy wrapped in a blanket, nursing at her breast. I quietly sat next to her as she barely opened her eyes.

"It's a boy."

It was a boy born in Alaska. We named him Jamie. Lucille stayed in the hospital for three days because of her heavy bleeding. I stayed with her, holding our new baby. Many friends visited, and I proudly showed him off.

Tiger Olsen was a few doors down from where Lucille and baby Jamie lay together. I visited him occasionally and struck up a friendship. Glad for the company, he shared stories about living alone at Taku Inlet. He had lived quite a life.

I brought my baby boy and placed him on Tiger's chest. He held him so tenderly, gently rubbing his little head with his rough, weathered hands. Looking down at this beautiful baby, Tiger sat up in his hospital bed as tears ran down his cheeks, dripping off his chin. He didn't want to let him go.

When it was time to return to our cabin, friends provided everything we needed to start our new life with our son. It was a joyful time. The little Indian girl living with us sat on the couch for hours, holding Jamie in her arms and kissing his forehead.

Wes Hanson

Wes Hansen was the happiest man I have ever met. He drove a bus for Juneau Municipal Bus Line. A regular visitor to the outreach house, he shared his remarkable story with me.

On his way home after finishing his shift, he was involved in a head-on collision. Technically, he died in the crash but remained aware of everything happening.

As his spirit left his body, he saw the crash site and the people who stopped to help. He found himself in the most beautiful valley, surrounded by a refreshing breeze. All his earthly worries were gone. Across a bubbling brook flowing through the valley, a fully blossomed green tree stood. In an instant, he was at the base of this tree, and a figure like Jesus stood before him.

He asked the figure, "Is it my time to go?"

Placing his hand on Wes's chest, tremendous energy surged through his body. He could only describe it as an infusion of pure love. It lasted so long he thought he might explode.

Finally, the figure said, "No, I'm sending you back for your family."

Wes said people on earth have no idea of the burdens we carry through life. He woke in a hospital bed in immense pain, once again engulfed by life's burdens.

He recovered, but two years later, his wife died of cancer. Shortly after, his son married a beautiful girl who became pregnant. At Thanksgiving dinner, his son's pregnant wife swallowed a turkey bone and began choking. She died on the floor before the ambulance could arrive.

When I left Alaska, Wes was still the happiest, most content man I'd ever met. He knew there was a heaven; he'd been there.

Return to California

Gospel Outreach changed while we were in Alaska. Teams were dispatched to various locations across the country, and outreach houses were established in Pomona, Sherman Oaks, and Anaheim, California, as well as in New York City, Boston, and Oswego, New York.

I joined the Mobile Ministers team, traveling to encourage outreach efforts at local houses.

The outreach houses supported themselves by starting businesses. The chosen enterprise was vinyl repair, which proved quite profitable. Working members would visit used car dealers to fix vinyl seats and dashboards, then return home and hand their earnings to the house elder, who paid the bills. The hardest part of vinyl repair was matching colors, but after some trial and error, they became proficient. Several vinyl repair teams earned so much money that temptation eventually got the best of them.

They left the house and started their own businesses. This was frowned upon by the leadership, but there wasn't much anyone could do about it. Later, it became usual for them to pay a tithe.

My first Mobile Minister trip was to Southern California. It was easy for Lucille and me because we stayed with her parents.

The Pomona house was in serious trouble. Situated in a predominantly Black neighborhood of Pomona, it faced hostility from residents who didn't welcome white people. It was a frightening place where gunshots often echoed through the night.

The week before we arrived, a white family a few doors down had an altercation with a group of locals that led to a drive-by shooting, shattering their front windows. They called the police, who came to investigate. Two nights later, someone threw a firebomb through their bedroom window where their baby was sleeping. The father rushed to rescue the baby and put out the fire. The next day, they moved out.

There was a break-in at the outreach house. An unusual couple managed the home—tall, nerdy, intellectual types with thick glasses. They took managing the house very seriously and weren't willing to give up easily.

Woken up one night by a commotion in the front room, they got up to investigate. Turning the corner, they found a large, older Black man rummaging through things, looking for something to steal. Realizing the man was extremely drunk, they rushed at him and knocked him to the floor.

The husband sat on his head, pinning his arms to the ground, while the wife grabbed his legs in a bear hug. When the intruder struggled to get free, she bit him on his ankle. Every time he moved, she bit harder. He finally gave up and lay there while they called the police.

Tent Revival on Sunset Strip

The Sherman Oaks outreach decided to host a tent revival on Sunset Strip in Hollywood. It was a significant event that required a lot of planning, and I was expected to participate. Several people came down from Eureka, including Jim Durkin.

The people of Sherman Oaks did an impressive job. They located an empty lot near the center of the Strip and arranged dates for a week-long event. They hired a company to set up a circus tent that covered the entire lot. They booked Christian bands and scripted skits with our people as actors. Several volunteers were prepared to share testimonies about how Christ had changed their lives for the better. A life-sized wooden cross was built for an actor dressed as Jesus to carry down Sunset Strip, depicting the crucifixion. People followed behind him, passing out flyers that advertised the evening's schedule at the tent. At the end of each night, Jim Durkin delivered a lively evangelical message and invited people to accept Jesus as their Savior.

The day finally arrived to begin the revival. Ron was chosen to kick things off by carrying the cross. He dressed in white linen with fake blood smeared across his back. With long hair and a beard, I've never seen a better Jesus.

He and his followers had just made it a block when a crowd started to gather. Many people were unsure what to think. Some believed it was part of a Hollywood production—strange theatrics and shenanigans always happened on that street.

Followers started handing out flyers, inviting people to the tent. Then, the situation began to spiral out of control. The crowd grew bigger and started to jeer and curse. The screaming and shouting drew an even larger crowd. People started throwing things at Ron and the cross. He did his best to keep going.

Some guy none of us knew started to chant, "HE CLAIMS TO BE THE SON OF GOD!" Every time he chanted, a loud "BOOOOOOO!" erupted from the crowd.

The crowd continued to grow, spilling into the street and blocking traffic, yelling, screaming, cursing, and throwing objects at Ron. The situation turned into a riot. The Sunset Strip locals didn't want Jesus on their street. It turned into chaos.

Police arrived first with one car, then two. Soon after, ten police cars showed up, officers jumping out, stopping traffic, and trying to understand what was happening. They moved through the crowd to a man dressed like Jesus carrying a large wooden cross and asked him what he was doing. Ron explained it was part of a week-long crusade and pointed to the tent down the road. The police were unimpressed and asked to see his permit. We didn't have one. That marked the end of the procession. We were escorted to the tent with a stern warning not to do that again, as we could have been cited for inciting a riot.

Carrying the cross on Sunset Strip turned into a fiasco, but it achieved the desired result. News quickly spread about the purpose of the big tent. Every night, a good crowd responded to the music, skits, testimonies, and the invitation to follow Jesus. Some people raised their hands for prayer and stood up in support of Jesus. A few ended up at the Lighthouse Ranch.

A Trip Back to the East Coast

During this period, Jesus People groups emerged spontaneously across the United States. As they grew, they looked for ways to establish their legitimacy without relying on traditional churches. The annual Jesus festivals offered many of these people the chance to meet Jim Durkin. If he approved, they would submit their group to Gospel Outreach. Jim helped guide them and granted the groups legitimacy.

Several groups were located in New England. A team was assembled to travel from Southern California to visit and support these groups, starting in New York City, then moving on to Boston, Utica, New York, and Oswego. We wrapped up our tour by spending the summer in New York City.

Transportation back east was by car. My family was one of the three families chosen, including a single person who played music. Traveling across the country, we stayed in campgrounds to save money. We gathered camping supplies, like tents and sleeping bags, and tied them to the roof of our cars. It was an adventure for most of us, as we had never been to the East Coast of America before.

Leaving Southern California, we headed east on Interstate 40 through Flagstaff, Albuquerque, Amarillo, Oklahoma City, Little Rock, Memphis, Nashville, and Knoxville. In Knoxville, we were to take Interstate 81 to visit the Civil War battle sites in the Shenandoah Valley.

Some nights we couldn't find a campground. We found a deserted place—not knowing whose property we were on—and set up camp. I slept uneasily those nights, thinking the cops would show up, but they never did.

We arrived in Staten Island late the next night and arranged to stay with people who graciously put us up. This was not a high-rolling operation. We stayed on floors, in basements, or wherever there was room. It was even more complicated with four little kids in tow, whose needs had to be met as well.

I had my first experience at a New York Diner on the East Coast!

Ministry in New York

In Brooklyn, where one group lived, they divided us up to stay with four different families. My family stayed in a pastor's house under the Verrazzano-Narrows Bridge.

The pastor was tall, thin, and very high-strung. His claim to fame was a child feeding program held in a small church not far from where we stayed. He spent the day constantly mistreating his Asian wife. No shortcoming escaped his criticism. Stoically enduring his abuse, she fed the children from the streets. To get away from it, we took long walks along the river, only showing up at mealtimes.

In the evenings, we went to local house group meetings and connected with the people we aimed to encourage. It was varied, but most were committed to reaching out and introducing others to Jesus.

I met Mario, an Italian guy remodeling a brownstone on Sterling Street in Bedford-Stuyvesant. It was meant to be a halfway house for people released from jail. Hearing about my construction background, he asked if I could help with the project. Wanting to get out of the situation under the bridge, I accepted his offer. We stayed at the "Brothers House" on 14th Avenue, just a few blocks from the project.

The Bedford-Stuyvesant neighborhood was the less-affluent part of Brooklyn, primarily African American, with a lot of street crime. The only white people I saw were at the "Brothers House."

David, an overamped, high-strung Jewish guy, ran the house. His father, a renowned heart surgeon, wanted David to follow in his footsteps and become a heart surgeon. He brought him into the operating room, having David participate in operations. David decided he'd rather do speed and heroin and dropped out. When he hit rock bottom, he visited the "Brothers House" and never left.

David was heading to the bank to deposit the weekly $400 earnings to support the brother's house. On the way, he passed by the local bookie. God told him to go inside and place a bet on number 14 in the next horse race. He obeyed God's voice, bet on 14, and walked out with $1,200.

David eventually moved to Lighthouse Ranch and married a girl named Mudgie. After leaving the ranch, he and Mudgie obtained their real estate licenses. They partnered with a Japanese investment group, acquiring properties in California. David and Mudgie became a very wealthy couple. David contracted liver cancer and passed away, leaving everything to Mudgie and their only son.

Brothers at the "Brothers House" worked at the New York shipyards. They had the worst job at the yard, moving supports inside the dry docks. It was dirty, miserable, hard work. As one ship left the dry dock, they muscled heavy supports around, getting ready for the next one. Sometimes they worked all night.

When they got home, they were dirty, tired, and hungry, but offered no complaints. They worked for a higher calling.

One night, a guy across the street had his speakers pointed out the window, blaring music as loud as they could go. The Brothers wanted to sleep before their next shift, but the music kept them awake. In desperation, a couple of brothers crossed the street to ask the guy to turn down the music.

The answer was, "GO FUCK YOURSELF!!"

Frustrated, they called the police to send down a squad car and tell the guy to turn down the music. The police's response left them speechless. The dispatcher explained they only came out for rape and murder that night. The music played on.

Walking to Sterling Street from the brothers' house, Mario would arrive and tell me to wait outside because he had to chain up the dog. He kept a dog there at night so nobody would break in and steal his tools and materials. The dog was the biggest, meanest, most vicious German Shepherd I'd ever seen. He was terrifying. Whenever anybody came near him, he would show his teeth and snarl with hate-filled eyes, go berserk, and try to break his chain. The only person who could get close was Mario.

The second day I arrived, two teenage boys were standing outside, angrier than hell. They asked me where the Italian guy was. I told them he'd be there shortly.

Mario showed up, and the two boys began cursing at him. Right away, they told him they had tried to break in through the roof the night before, and the dog almost attacked them. They said that if he didn't get rid of that dog, there would be trouble. Mario told them that's why he had the dog and told them to get lost. The boys lingered for a while, complaining some more, until he opened the front door. The dog stuck its head out, and Mario put a leash on it so he could take it out to relieve itself. The two boys ran off, their faces filled with terror.

The halfway house was a three-story brownstone built in the early nineteen-twenties. A lot of work had been completed before I arrived. It was ready to hang the doors. Mario asked if I knew how to hang doors, and I told him I could. I hung seven doors on my first day. Mario was impressed with the work and asked if I could stay on to help him finish the project. I was scheduled to stay with a family in Queens the following weekend. Between the dog, attempted break-ins, and loud music, I didn't change my schedule.

Our next visit to George and Maria's home in Queens was a pleasant break. The house was tidy and inviting. George and Maria's two well-behaved children were polite. They addressed us as Mr. and Mrs. Means—a novelty coming from California.

Maria's cooking was exceptional. They introduced us to New York bagels—what a delight! A toasted onion bagel with cream cheese stole my heart. I couldn't get enough of them.

Maria's spaghetti carbonara was the best I'd ever had. They went out of their way to make us feel comfortable. They turned us onto JR's Cheesecake restaurant in downtown New York. My favorite was cherry cheesecake.

That became a regular stop when we went into the city.

George was the top sales representative for Panasonic. He succeeded in providing well for himself and his family. Maria came from a large Italian family. Her father was a New York lawmaker who had been prepared to run for president. Maria's father was kidnapped by the Mafia and held for ransom. The Mafia eventually released him, and he went on to serve as a New York Supreme Court judge.

George and Maria introduced us to their friends, Bob and Alice Smith. Bob owned a large flooring business, and he and Alice lived in an exclusive housing development in Freeport, Long Island.

Bob's favorite pastime was playing tennis. He and Alice belonged to a private pool and tennis club. In conversation, he mentioned he had a tennis match the next day. Lucille noted that she had been a tennis player and was quite good. Before she came to the Lighthouse Ranch, her family belonged to a tennis club in Southern California, and she played in tournaments. She was so talented that many thought she should turn pro.

Bob got excited when he heard this and asked if we could stay with them. He wanted to take Lucille to his club, introduce her to the members, and watch her play.

George and Maria encouraged us to go, thinking Lucille would enjoy herself. It didn't take much for us to agree, so we packed up and drove to Freeport.

Bob and Alice had a lovely home in a waterfront community with a swimming pool and a path leading down to a canal with a boat dock. The tennis club was part of the community and featured a large marina.

Lucille's debut at the tennis club was a hit. She crushed the competition and quickly gained popularity. Afterward, these high-rolling ladies and men lined up to meet her. They wanted to schedule times to play with her.

At Bob's house, the phone rang nonstop with people asking where he had found this girl. Bob was as proud as a peacock; Lucille loved the admiration. A women's doubles tournament was scheduled for next week, so he added her name to the list.

Two More Stops

Lucille and her tennis partner won their doubles match, but it was time to move on. Our next stop was Boston, Massachusetts. In Boston, we stayed with Neil and Annie Warner. Neil and Annie were house group leaders for Gospel Outreach Boston, but our relationship had been ongoing for a few years. They were former hippies who became Jesus people at Sabina's Land in California, where Lucille and I had been the leaders.

Annie was a charming, cultured girl with a great personality. She wore hippie clothes that were always fresh and clean, and her hair was well-kept. She came from Boston, where her father, an architect and artist, had made a name for himself.

Neil was a Vietnam veteran who served with the Navy SEALs. Neil and I shared an unspoken bond as veterans.

When we met, they were boyfriend and girlfriend. When they became followers of Jesus, they felt it was appropriate to get married.

Because I was the leader of Sabina's Land, they asked me to marry them. I was ordained through Gospel Outreach, which gave me the authority to perform marriages.

As the wedding day neared, her father and mother flew in from Boston. Annie had chosen a spot for her wedding on a bluff overlooking the Pacific Ocean—a beautiful location when the weather was nice. But on her wedding day, the weather was far from pleasant.

It was cold and dark, with a gale blowing and occasional rain showers. Annie was determined to have her wedding on the bluff regardless, so we bundled up and headed out. The wind was so fierce we could hardly open the car doors.

The wedding party gathered on the bluff, leaning into the wind. It started to rain, with the wind blowing so hard it stung our faces. Annie's parents, clutching their coats and soaked, struggled to stay upright. They didn't look happy on this supposedly joyful occasion. I cut the ceremony short and pronounced them husband and wife. After a quick kiss, we hurried back to the cars for the reception at the big house. Annie's father handed me twenty bucks.

Even with a rough start, Neil and Annie's marriage ultimately proved to be a success. They stayed together until Neil died of a heart attack while working in his garden.

***

We enjoyed our time in Boston visiting the historical sites. However, I was starting to get tired of group house meetings. Homesick and weary of staying in other people's homes, we still had to visit Paul and Polly Wagner in Oswego, upstate New York.

Paul and Polly made a lovely couple. Paul was an anthropology professor at Oswego State University. A Harrison Ford lookalike with a goatee, he was the heartthrob of his female students.

We drove through the rural farmlands of upstate New York, stopping briefly in Utica to visit a group house. I never realized how beautiful the New York countryside could be, dotted with small, charming villages, their white church steeples rising above the trees. I was especially captivated by Oswego, nestled beside Lake Ontario with a pre-revolutionary fort. We arrived on a warm summer day for a picnic Paul was hosting on the lake. People were friendly, and the food was excellent.

Paul was invited to lead the Anthropology Department at Oswego University after he had lived in a remote Amazon Indian village surrounded by the jungles of Brazil. With Polly accompanying him, they lived among the jungle natives, studying the traditions of their hosts for a couple of years. Paul was using that experience to write a dissertation for his PhD.

Polly had to pull Paul out of the jungle after he got jungle fever that nearly killed him. She never wanted to go there in the first place, so it didn't break her heart.

Initially, I met Paul at the Lighthouse Ranch. He became a Jesus person right after he ended an affair with one of his students. It had been a tough time for Paul and Polly as they struggled to keep their marriage together. Paul was a natural-born leader. His charisma drew people to him. After his conversion, he soon hosted meetings for Jesus' people at his home. He heard about the Lighthouse Ranch, and he and Polly drove across the country in their VW Bug, towing a tent trailer to investigate.

I hosted them during their visit to Eureka and introduced them to the leadership. They seemed like sure choices for a cooperation agreement. His group became Gospel Outreach Oswego.

His becoming a Jesus person didn't sit well with Paul's academic colleagues. They tried to have him expelled from campus. Paul fought back and kept his position, but not without ongoing conflicts and turmoil.

His popular course with students generated a significant amount of money for the university.

Back to California Again

After our trip to Oswego, I was determined to go back to California. When I told my fellow travelers I needed to go back, they looked at me in disbelief. Lucille was mad at me because she wanted to play more tennis. It was a long trip home, and I received silent treatment. Driving back to Eureka from New York, I knew I was in trouble. Lucille was mad at me, and I had to answer to the leadership.

Deep down, I was disappointed with myself. It was one of those things I had to do. I couldn't pull out of my emotional funk and was still searching for some relief. I didn't realize that I was addicted to adrenaline. People with this addiction need some crisis. Without a crisis, you feel useless and bored to the point of being sick. I was sick. In the war, being constantly on adrenaline high had become the norm. Adrenaline is a heavy drug. I felt like a puppet on a string, and adrenaline was the puppet master.

In Eureka, we initially stayed with friends of ours, John and Sharon Omey. John was a successful dentist. They lived in a substantial Victorian home. Their house had burned down a few years earlier, with their oldest daughter trapped in her bedroom.

Sharon bravely faced the flames, rushing up the stairs and grabbing her daughter. She kicked out the bedroom window and jumped from the second story with her daughter in her arms. Both survived, bruised and sore. Sharon was a true hero. John and Sharon rebuilt their home to perfect condition, adding extra bedrooms.

John and my family go way back. Originally, John was from Long Beach. After my dad left the Navy, he started his own construction company with John's dad doing the plumbing.

John finished dental school and moved to Eureka, where he started his practice. John and Sharon, impressed with the Lighthouse Ranch, got involved in supporting the outreach work. His contribution was providing free dental care to the Jesus People's teeth.

We ran into each other at a meeting. He approached me and asked if I was Bob Means and whether my father served on PT boats during the war. I confirmed, and he explained that our fathers had worked together. Ten years older than me, he remembered me as a small, towheaded kid working on my dad's construction jobs while he worked for his father.

Sharon passed away with Alzheimer's this year—a significant loss.

Returning from New York, it didn't take long for my true feelings to show to those around me. I became a pain in the ass, a fly in the ointment.

There was a house group in San Diego that had connected with Gospel Outreach. I found my escape when one of our couples moved there, and Lucille and I went with them.

San Diego

We moved into a condo in Carlsbad that my dad had available. My brother worked for a landscaper, and they needed a maintenance foreman, so I took on the job of managing the maintenance crews. The next step was to buy a surfboard and get back to surfing. I was a bit out of practice, but I quickly regained my old form. Then I reconnected with old friends from San Clemente and went on a surfing trip down to Baja, Mexico.

Camping on the beach, I was back in my element and loving it.

Lucille went to the doctor and found out she was pregnant again. At the same time, we learned her dad had a brain tumor and wasn't expected to survive. Between her pregnancy and her father's crisis, she was an emotional wreck. When her father passed away, she was overwhelmed with grief.

A New Job - A New Home - A New Son

Johnny, the house group leader in San Diego, informed me about an opening with Schrock Construction, which specializes in installing house foundations. The attractive part of this job was that it was unionized, meaning I would get union-level pay, along with medical and dental benefits, and vacation pay. I applied and was hired.

We left the condo in Carlsbad and moved to Clairemont Mesa, where we found an apartment above Mission Bay. It was closer to my work, and our old friends, Larry and Lynn Johnson, lived up the street. Larry Johnson had overseen the Clark and B Street house in Eureka.

San Diego was a fantastic place to live. A continuous building boom created lots of work. I bought a small 14-foot sailboat so I could go sailing on Mission Bay when the surf was flat.

I left Schrock Construction and started doing piecework. Framing walls paid $0.07 per square foot, and I earned $100 a day. I later made $200 for hanging fascia. I was asked to build staircases for large condo and apartment complexes. They paid one hundred dollars per set, and I could install four sets a day. That's $400 a day! I was making good money!

Our second son, Christopher, was born in a San Diego hospital without any complications. Lucille made many good friends. With plenty of money and great weather, why would anyone want to live anywhere else?

Off to Hawaii

I met a family building a ferrocement sailboat in Santee, east of San Diego. Building ferrocement boats was a fad at the time. It was promoted as a way to make an affordable, ocean-going sailboat in your backyard using chicken wire and cement, then sail off into the sunset. Most that I saw were poorly built. Ninety percent never got finished and ended up in the trash heap.

But this family was different; they were on a mission with a Christian group. Their boat was sailing to the South Pacific to reach remote islands and preach the gospel. This sounded exciting, so I volunteered to help. It satisfied my need to keep my adrenaline up. Lucille was not enthusiastic.

Allan Williams, based in Hawaii, led the small boat ministry and visited the project. During our conversation, he told me that several boats and families dedicated to this effort were located on the Big Island of Hawaii. I mentioned that I was certified in water survival and could teach the families and crews. He liked the idea and asked if I would come to Hawaii to teach water survival to his people. This invitation set off a series of events for me and my family. I was committed from the start, and I had to convince the rest of the family to join me.

Life in San Diego was comfortable, but when I told Allan I needed work on the island, he arranged a job helping one of his friends build his dream house. It came together miraculously. I bought a plane ticket to the Big Island and shipped my truck over. I ordered a new surfboard from my friend's surf shop. I wouldn't want to go out without a new board!

Landing at the Big Island airport, Allan, his wife Fay, their two young boys, Scott Shoot, and his wife were waiting for me. It was Scott's house I was going to build.

Allan was an Englishman from Liverpool. In his early years, he was often intoxicated and enjoyed getting into bar fights. He found religion and changed his ways. Shortly after moving to New Zealand, he met Fay and married her. They took a mission post in the Cook Islands and then learned about work in Hawaii. Moving there, they were put in charge of the small boat ministry.

Later, Allan found out he had heart problems. He and Fay moved back to New Zealand for medical treatment. One day, he collapsed and died while out jogging.

Scott was a wild Canadian hippie from Toronto who moved to Hawaii to do drugs and relax on the beach. Burned out on drugs, he found religion and joined a mission group. He fell in love, got married, and inherited a large sum of money. Moving out of the commune, he was ready to build their house. Scott changed his name to David after King David, as mentioned in the Bible. Several fire-breathing Christians also changed their names to biblical patriarchs.

I stayed with Allan and Fay until I found my own place. Their room was in an old resort up the hill overlooking Kailua-Kona. The mission group had purchased this rundown resort to transform it into a Bible training center, with a focus on outreach to the Pacific Islands.

Daytime activities involved working on the old buildings between prayer times and Bible readings. As a guest, I was exempt from the rules and had the freedom to find a place to bring my family.

At the bottom of the hill, a large apartment complex had vacancies. I rented a two-bedroom apartment and called my family to come over. My truck arrived along with my carpenter tools. I went to work on Scott's house, which is high on the mountain. I hadn't even thought about bringing warm clothes to a tropical island, but on the first day of work, I froze my butt off. Scott liked my work, and we got along well.

Then I met Bob, a close friend of Scott's. Bob was a local carpenter working for Dennis Heidi, building exclusive homes. He had lived on the island for years and knew everyone. Bob was invaluable in showing me the ropes of doing construction on an island, where materials had to be shipped in from the mainland, and it wasn't easy finding what you needed.

Bob had a harelip and wasn't particularly good-looking, but he had a pretty and headstrong wife. I could tell their marriage was in bad shape and figured it wasn't going to last much longer. Bob and I had met before, from a distance. He was in Vietnam serving with the Navy Seabees. His first night in Vietnam was the first night of the Tet Offensive. His base was on the other side of the Han River from the bridge ramp, where twenty Army guys and I were engaged with Viet Cong. They issued him an M16 rifle and sent him to an outpost. While we were fighting off the enemy, our bullets flew across the river, hitting their position. I told him some of those bullets coming at him were mine. I would've hated killing Bob—he was a nice guy, and I told him so.

My family arrived and settled into our new apartment. I can't say they were happy, especially Lucille. She didn't see a future in what we were doing. People in Hawaii are transient—here today, gone tomorrow. When you first arrive, it feels like you've entered paradise. But it doesn't take long before the island starts to feel claustrophobic. Lucille hit it off with Scott's and Bob's wives, who had a long list of frustrations and were eager to find someone to listen. Lucille became their confidante, quickly overwhelmed by their problems. I wanted to go surfing.

With thirty participants, Allan and I organized the first water survival course. We gathered at the Kailua-Kona pier for verbal instructions and dry land practice drills. The participants took it very seriously, eager to get in the water to hone their new skills.

Lining up on the edge of the pier, they assumed the jump position. When given the command to "jump," they plunged into the water with a splash. A crowd gathered on the pier, wondering what was happening. For the next hour, they stayed in the water practicing water survival techniques. I watched along with the growing crowd from the pier. After an hour in the water, the students were excited. They had passed and learned how to take care of themselves if needed.

The first class was a booming success. But trouble was brewing with the small boat concept due to a lack of funds. The idea would soon be abandoned, and there I sat with my family in Hawaii, far from home.

I finished Scott's house and got a job with Dennis Heidi, working with Bob to build a large estate overlooking Napapoe Bay, where Captain Cook was killed by natives in the early 1800s. I surfed on weekends with Bob's surfer friends, who showed me the local surf spots.

Surfing on the Big Island is scary. Good surf spots have gnarly bottom of jagged coral or lava runoffs. Wiping out was a nasty way to get hurt, so being selective about which wave to take off on minimized the fun. Sharks were also an issue—I kept an eye out for the black tips. Most shark attacks came from these monsters.

Free diving was another sport my new friends shared with me. Our favorite spot was on the coral edge, a half-mile out in Napapoe Bay. The coral was eight feet deep until it reached the shelf, then dropped to eighty feet. It was spectacular looking over this edge and diving down to forty feet among lots of fish and brilliant colors.

They showed me how to dive to eighty feet. At these depths, the pressure of the water against your lungs made you feel like you didn't need a breath of air. I had to remind myself to go up and get air constantly. The frightening part was that when you turned and looked out to sea, the water dropped down 13,000 feet. The ocean went from dark blue to black, and out there were multiple species of sharks.

Ben was a true adventurer until he got the bends while diving off Easter Island. He had built a beautiful schooner out of ferrocement that he planned to charter from Long Beach, California. During the construction, a Coast Guard inspector needed to be present to oversee the cement application to approve a charter license. The inspector was late. Ben didn't wait; his cement was mixed, and he didn't want to waste the batch. The inspector arrived just as he was finishing. Consequently, Ben was denied his charter certificate.

Unfazed, Ben sailed his schooner to Valparaíso, Chile, to organize trips to Easter Island. While diving for lobster with a full catch, he realized his time was up and surfaced, leaving his lobsters on the seabed. Back on deck, he felt good and thought he could dive again to retrieve his bag.

Halfway down, he blacked out and woke up in the Valparaíso hospital, paralyzed from the waist down.

His crew, realizing he was in trouble, called SOS and dove down to rescue him. A Chilean frigate was in the area, and divers from the ship took him back down to decompress for hours, changing his tanks and mouthpiece as necessary. They saved his life but not his legs.

Ben ended up in Hawaii, living in an old warehouse, hobbling along on crutches, and unable to control his bladder. When I met him, he heard I was a carpenter and asked if I could help him build a small boat from a set of plans so he could go sailing again. I agreed, and before long, Ben was back at sea, and we became friends.

Ben still enjoyed diving. I would take him into the water and help him with a mask and snorkel. He'd observe the sea life while floating on the surface, his legs hanging freely. I would go with him, and when he'd had enough, I'd carry him onto the beach, place him in the car, and drive him back to his warehouse.

One afternoon, I received a call from Ben asking to dive at Napapoe Bay. Although it was getting late, I agreed, and we set out. As I prepared to help Ben into the water from the small concrete dock, I noticed local fishermen cleaning a fresh catch of yellowfin tuna. They were dumping buckets of bloody water into the bay. I mentioned this to Ben, wondering if it was a good idea to go diving with blood in the water. Ben decided it would be fine, so I helped him in and dove in after him.

It was a great day for diving. The water was clear as Ben made his way to the edge of the reef, his legs swinging freely. Staying close to Ben, I noticed a large coral head with several brightly colored purple fish darting in and out. I dove down to get a closer look. Coming up for air near the surface, two eight-foot reef sharks swam past on either side of me. They had smelled the fish blood and were searching for a meal.

Desperately fighting off panic and staying focused, I followed the plan step by step. Slowly, I moved toward the beach, keeping my eyes on these two sharks cruising the bay.

Reaching the beach, I felt immense relief, then realized I had forgotten about Ben, his legs dangling like perfect shark bait. My heart pounded, and a lump formed in my throat when I knew I needed to get to him. For a moment, I thought about leaving him to his own devices. I didn't want to go back into that water. After all, he had wanted to go in knowing there was blood in the water.

Reluctantly, I put on my fins and slowly swam toward Ben, who was well out in the bay. Now eight black tips were circling. I reached Ben and asked if he'd noticed the sharks. He was ready to go in. With Ben on his back and my arm over his chest, clutching his armpit, we slowly moved toward the beach, wondering which one of us would get bitten first. I was ecstatic when my feet touched down in the shallow water. Picking up Ben, I carried him to the car.

There was an excellent body-surfing spot down the coast that only broke when waves came from the southwest. One Saturday morning, Scott heard it was breaking and called to see if I wanted to go. Scott only body-surfed, and I agreed to join him. When we arrived, the waves were breaking at about five feet. Putting on our fins, we headed out through the break, catching peaks and surfing both ways—right and left—wave after wave.

The waves were getting bigger and started closing out. I caught a large one with nowhere to go and ducked my head down to roll through the impact zone. The bottom dropped out, and I landed headfirst on the hard sandy floor. Immediately, I knew I had hurt my neck. Crawling to the beach, I sat there feeling uneasy, a bit shaken. I thought maybe I had a slight concussion. Struggling to the car, I told Scott I had injured myself.

When I got home, I went to bed, not knowing I had broken my neck.

It took eight years to find out.

Breakdown

At this point, my reason for moving to Hawaii had fallen apart, and we were basically just stuck there with no clear purpose. My family wasn't happy. So many people came and went that it was hard for Lucille to keep friendships. The island was starting to feel overwhelming, and my ongoing depression began to return.

Then it happened. I went upstairs to take a shower and started speaking gibberish, unable to cope anymore, falling apart mentally and emotionally. An overwhelming fear took over my body, mind, and spirit. I had a complete nervous breakdown. I knew immediately that the war in Vietnam had finally caught up to me.

My family was caught in the middle. They never wanted to be in Hawaii in the first place. I became catatonic, unable to speak, sitting on the couch, too afraid to go to the bathroom. I tried going to work, but that was pure hell too. Nobody could figure out what had come over me. I wasn't sure what had happened to me either. At work, Bob cussed me out, thinking I was being an asshole. All I could do was take it.

I had to get off that island.

Moving back to San Diego, I tried to work but couldn't keep up with my responsibilities. We drove back to Eureka and rented a house through the state housing program, trying to get my life and mental health back on track. I found menial work to support the household. I started attending church and rereading my Bible. I reached out to my old friends for help, but I had become a nuisance, and they pulled away from me.

A friend came down from Alaska to visit the church in Eureka. He was a Vietnam vet. We got together one afternoon, and I shared what I was going through. He had experienced the same thing and shared his story with me. Finally, I found someone to confide in, someone who understood. We talked for what felt like hours, and I felt a sense of relief in opening up. It took him three years to get back to normal, including temporary relapses that became less frequent over time. I wasn't looking forward to this hanging on for years, but at least I hoped I would be stable again someday.

I went to a bookstore and bought every book I could find on nervous breakdowns. It was a relief to realize I wasn't alone, and the information in the books guided my recovery. I learned that a nervous breakdown was caused by anger and rage. The Marines taught me to be angry and full of rage—enough to kill innocent people if necessary in combat. I read that a breakdown should really be called a breakup; it's a reset of your emotions to rebuild. Ultimately, it took three years to recover fully. I struggled to keep the family fed and sheltered.

I learned about life cycles from a book and then began to experience them firsthand. My life followed thirty-day cycles. My mental struggles could get so severe that I had to stay in bed for a couple of days. Then the pressure would lessen, and I would gradually start to recover until I felt better and at peace. After a few days, I would enter another downward cycle until I needed to go back to bed. I started noticing these cycles and realized I could handle the tough ones, knowing the good periods would return in a few days.

The destructive cycles decreased, and the positive ones improved, almost returning to normal. I recovered from my illness after three years of hardship. This rage was going to be in me for my entire life because of the war. I was obsessed, and to recover I had to get involved once again in something bigger than myself.

The process took a severe toll on my family, which proved to be irreversible.

From Rage to Courage

Sailing on Schooner *So Fong*, Vietnam

Recovery and a New Calling

A major earthquake struck Guatemala, causing extensive destruction. Several Spanish-speaking members of our group formed a team to travel to the area and assist with rebuilding efforts. They repaired schools and bridges. A close friend, Bob Trolese, was appointed to oversee the largest housing project ever constructed in the region.

The group started a new church that quickly gained members. I kept hearing stories about their work and became more interested. I decided to visit and see for myself.

I got a job at Rainbow Mini Storage in Eureka, where I built hundreds of storage units and made a decent living. I saved money, applied for a passport, and bought a ticket on Pan Am Airways to Guatemala City, thinking there might be an opportunity for me with my construction skills.

When I arrived, the church had expanded to 7,000 members. Among them were three of the most influential families in Guatemala. Their participation drew in many more wealthy families. It was a growing issue that significantly altered the country's political landscape.

Several friends met me. Over the next few days, they invited me to join them and shared their accomplishments. I was genuinely impressed. The worship meetings were lively, filled with energetic Latin worship music and dancing in the aisles. Being a dancer myself, I eagerly joined in.

I caught up with an old friend, Wally Sharp. He had run a small youth outreach in Grants Pass, Oregon, when I first met him. He and his wife wanted to start an orphanage, and moving to Latin America gave him the opportunity. He had fifteen orphans living in a large house on the outskirts of Guatemala City.

Spending the day with him, he explained that he needed a bigger place and was looking at land in a community south of the city called San José Penula. He wanted to build a facility to house these children, and I told him I would like to help him bring his vision to life. Here was the very thing I needed for my recovery. I had the skills to make this happen. It was definately bigger than myself.

After I returned home, I spoke with a local architect and asked if he could help design a building for fifty children. The architect was Mormon and took on the project to serve his God. He drew up a set of plans at no charge. We conducted a cost analysis and found that the project would cost around $80,000 at US prices to complete.

That gave me a starting point and the beginning of a new life—something bigger than myself. I had my family to worry about, but I believed God would handle that part of my life if I helped the poor. In the end, it didn't turn out that way.

We planned to build volunteer construction teams from our network of outreaches and churches that we had connected with. Team members would be responsible for raising their own funds for transportation, living expenses while in the country, and an additional $200 for construction materials. We intended to use ten-person teams for ten days each. Wally arranged for room and board, as well as in-country transportation, once the teams arrived.

To launch this venture, the response was incredible. Churches and individuals from the United States and Canada expressed interest in participating. Team members were chosen from the applications. Our first team's task was to dig the foundation trenches and pour the building's footings.

The day finally arrived for our first adventure. Each team member traveled from their hometown and met at the Houston airport for the flight to Guatemala. Everyone was excited, with some feeling a little nervous. I was in my element as the team members bonded.

The two-hour flight from Houston to Guatemala went smoothly. The weather was perfect when we landed at the Guatemala airport. We cleared customs while Wally waited in the lobby with a bus outside. He had planned for the team to stay at the big house with the orphans.

The ride through Guatemala City lasted as long as the flight. For most team members, this was their first visit to a developing country. Seeing extreme poverty up close was a sobering wake-up call.

When we got to the big house, the orphans greeted us warmly. Naturally, the women on the team couldn't wait to get off the bus and hug them. It was love at first sight. Tears flowed openly. It was going to be crowded in the big house with the orphans and our team. Sleeping arrangements consisted of mats on the floor with sleeping bags. The toilet facilities were subpar.

While we stored our gear, the staff set out a meal around a large table: black bean soup with corn tortillas in plastic bowls and cups. As delicious as it was, the Guatemalan coffee was a favorite. Most team members had one of the orphans sitting on their laps as they ate.

Work was divided between skilled and unskilled workers. Everyone was given a task and felt they contributed to a noble cause. After ten days, the foundation footings were dug, the rebar was set, and the foundation was poured. It was a significant achievement. Although the team was successful, after ten days, they were ready to go home.

Over the next year, I assembled many teams and stayed with each one until the new buildings were completed and Wally and his kids moved in.

Feeling good about starting a new chapter in my life, I was in my element. However, my family, especially Lucille, thought that they were overlooked. Bitterness crept in as I was pulled into this new path.

The Nicaragua Housing Project

The Verbo church had grown to astonishing numbers, but with that growth came problems. Leaders competed for more prominent positions, and rivalry was widespread.

Bob Trolese married a girl on the team and wanted to go to Nicaragua to start an outreach after the Sandinistas won the war against Somoza. The leadership didn't want him to go, but he had inherited the necessary funds and went anyway.

Nicaragua was a mess, a trash heap torn apart by war. The Russians and Cubans were running the place without funds. Talented people had fled to Miami to start businesses there. Grocery stores sat empty except for rows of Cuban rum. Bob's wife gave birth to their first child there, and at the hospital where their baby girl was born, they were sent to a room with a cot and dirty bed sheets.

That didn't stop them from setting up a small outreach. Bob was joined by Alfred and his wife, who traveled from Guatemala to help get things started. Alfred was a German-Guatemalan. His family had migrated to Central America in the mid-1800s to take advantage of the region's rich resources and start export businesses to Europe. Generations later, these Germans had become part of Guatemalan culture.

A small group of Christian Creole boys from the Miskito Coast traveled to Managua to attend school. They were motivated to help rebuild their country after the war's disruption, but they lacked direction and funds.

Bob and Alfred filled that gap, working together on small projects in their local area. Some of these boys were talented musicians, and after a hard day's work, they often started playing music. The lively Latin beat attracted people from the neighborhood, and a small beginning grew into a strong fellowship.

Bob visited the States and stayed with Lucille and me. He explained that the new Sandinista government was making things hard for missionaries. The latest order was that missionaries not involved in major redevelopment projects had to leave. I suggested starting a housing project, like one he had done in Guatemala. He liked the idea, and we made a plan.

I committed to raising money for 100 shelters and purchasing the necessary materials. Due to the numerous problems and material shortages there, we decided it would be easier to ship them in.

Bob met with the Nicaraguan government about land acquisition and legal matters. I didn't realize at the time how significant this project would be, but it felt good, and I was excited to get started.

After completing my work at the orphanage in Guatemala, I established a group of supporters who followed my activities and provided both financial and physical support. This project in Nicaragua gave them another chance to get involved.

Right away, I ran into a roadblock with the leadership at the Church in Eureka. When I suggested the idea of a housing project in Nicaragua, they rolled their eyes. They sat me down and told me this was a stupid idea, called me a dreamer, and said I could never pull off such an endeavor. They wouldn't support me.

Undeterred, I set out to prove them wrong. Without their support, I had to find external supporters to make this happen.

I got started in earnest. Many people I contacted were already familiar with Bob and eager to join in. I was encouraged by their response.

I designed a small, twelve-foot-by-sixteen-foot shelter with corrugated metal roofing. We planned to produce one hundred units, calculated the materials needed for each, and then multiplied that by one hundred. When I checked with the local lumber yard I had worked with for years, they agreed to give me a discount because of the humanitarian situation.

Funds to build 100 units totaled $56,000, plus a 10% contingency fee.

The Nicaraguan government approved the project easily. A piece of land was allocated for the community. People in this community lived in a shanty town with homes made from cardboard boxes and plastic roofs. Bob said one house had the hood of a 1953 Chevy as a roof.

Finding a Ship

The magnitude hadn't fully registered yet. I had hundreds of appeal letters to send to everyone I knew, explaining the situation and the project's scope. After setting up a tax-deductible account, donations began to come in gradually.

But how could I get materials to Nicaragua? I needed a ship. Where could I find a cargo vessel? I checked several shipping agents, but the costs were too high. Many companies have refused to operate in Nicaragua due to the country's political instability and uncertainty.

I read about the first missionaries to Hawaii. Later generations cultivated pineapples on the islands, and to transport their fruit, they established a shipping company called Castle and Cooke.

Castle and Cooke continued to operate in the shipping industry, with its headquarters in San Francisco. They had shipped bananas from Nicaragua before the revolution. I called the main office, explained our vision, and requested a meeting with someone who could assist with shipping materials to Nicaragua. The woman I spoke to said she would investigate it and get back to me within a few days. I was amazed that they would take the time to talk to me. Two days later, I received a call saying they would meet with me the following week. I paused for a moment after the call. Was this really happening?

On the day of the meeting, I got up early to drive the five hours from Eureka to San Francisco. I wasn't nervous; I figured I would present my case and see what happened. I had nothing to lose.

In San Francisco, with some extra time, I located their high-rise building and parked in the underground garage. At the reception desk, I provided my name and explained the reason for my visit.

I was politely told to take the elevator to the top floor to meet Captain Shorn, the company's CEO.

When the elevator opened, I found myself in a large room facing Captain Shorn's secretary's desk. She was standing at the elevator door to greet me. We shook hands and introduced ourselves, then she led me to Captain Shorn's office. The atmosphere was very friendly, and I felt entirely at ease.

Captain Shorn began the conversation by asking about my background and how I became involved in this project. I provided a brief overview of my life, starting with my time in the Marines and my experiences in Vietnam. My conversion experience, followed by the story of the project in Guatemala after the earthquake, the orphanage effort, and how Bob ended up in Nicaragua. I explained the need for this housing project and how Bob wanted to stay in Nicaragua to continue his mission work. I also described the progress we made in obtaining government approval in Nicaragua, as well as our fundraising efforts.

After my presentation, Shorn shared a bit of his background with me. He had been a sea captain working with Castle and Cooke, skippering one of their ships. From there, he advanced to become the company's CEO. He told me about the company's history and mission heritage. They were sympathetic to mission groups.

He paused quietly, contemplating. I felt we had established a connection. He looked at me and said he would dedicate one of his ships to the project free of charge.

Stunned, I blurted out, "Thank you!"

He explained they needed a month's notice to divert one of their ships from their Caribbean operation and bring it into the port of Long Beach. Before we went much further, I would have to get permission from the longshoremen in Long Beach to load the ship as a donation. Since there was no profit to be made, his company didn't want to pay the longshoremen's fees. That last statement went over my head. I was in awe that they gave me a ship for free!

Driving home, I thought about how I might persuade those longshoremen to load the ship for free. The union of the longshoremen was strong and fiercely protected its members, making it a tough—maybe impossible—challenge. Then it hit me—my Uncle Vic had spent his entire life as a longshoreman at the Long Beach docks.

I called Mom to get Uncle Vic's phone number. I hadn't seen or talked to him since my Aunt June died of leukemia years earlier. Mom told me he had become a recluse after June's death and hadn't kept in touch with the family. He had turned bitter, numbing his wounds with alcohol. I wondered if getting his help might be more complicated than getting the ship for free.

Before calling him, I wanted to check on the progress of the funding appeal. Upon checking the account, the total balance was $8,000. That made me nervous. Money was coming in slowly, in small amounts. Maybe the church leadership was right; perhaps I was a dreamer.

Checking the account two or three times a day caused so much stress that I decided to take a two-week break from reviewing it and focus on the tasks that needed to be done. We hadn't bought anything that cost money yet; everything was still in the planning stage. If we failed, I would refund the donors. My time was free.

Putting funding issues aside, I called my uncle. He answered the phone in his slow, deep voice, clearly surprised to hear from me. I asked him how he was doing; he replied that he wasn't doing so well. This wasn't going to be easy. Getting right to the point, I explained why I called, asking if he knew who I should call at the longshoremen's union to move forward with the project.

After a long silence, he told me the name of Jose Garcia, the union leader, along with his phone number. I wrote it down and thanked him. My Uncle Vic died a few months later.

When I called the number, I asked to speak with Jose Garcia. I was surprised that they connected me right away — I had Jose on the other end of the line! I told him my uncle gave me his number. He said he knew my uncle well and asked how he could help me. This was going way too smoothly.

I explained the humanitarian effort in Nicaragua and mentioned that I had acquired a ship from Castle and Cooke, which agreed to transport the materials for free. To reach our goal, the longshoreman would need to load the ship as a donation.

Without hesitation, he said he would bring this request to the members at the next meeting and asked if I would come to give a presentation. I agreed, and he provided me with the time and date, which was a week away. I told him I would be there.

It occurred to me that we could pull this off. I might travel to Nicaragua to build a hundred houses.

Packing up the family again, we drove twelve hours to Tustin. It was an excellent opportunity to visit family while attending to some business.

On the day of the meeting, a friend of mine, Bernie Harldson, asked if he could come along. Moral support would be helpful, so I agreed. This was new and strange to me, completely unbelievable. I was familiar with the harbor district and found the union office easily. After introducing ourselves to the receptionist, she took us to Jose's office.

Jose was friendly and asked us to sit down, explaining how the meeting would proceed. After handling the usual business with the group, we would present our request and then step outside while the members voted. I thanked him for his time and the opportunity to meet with the union.

He said, "No problem," and then entered the conference hall.

We waited in the lobby until Jose leaned out the door and invited us inside. He quickly introduced himself and asked me to deliver my presentation to the members. Twenty union members sat around a large table when I began speaking. I told them about our project and explained that I would need their help to make it happen.

After I finished my presentation, Jose led us back into the lobby. The vote didn't take long. When asked to return to the hall, Jose announced that the vote was in favor of our request. However, we still needed permission from the Stevedore company to use their equipment.

Unfamiliar with how the system operated, Jose explained that the stevedore company secures the contract to load ships and hires longshoremen from the hall to handle the loading. The equipment, including forklifts and loading straps, belongs to the Stevedore company. Jose gave me the name and address of the company and asked me to notify him once we had approval.

We thanked them and then went to find the Stevedore company's office. I was excited about the results of the union meeting. I believed the Stevedore company wouldn't cause any problems after our success. It almost ended up sabotaging the entire project.

I contacted the Stevedore company and scheduled an appointment. The owner was very gracious and supportive of our project. He allowed us to proceed but told us we needed liability insurance. His insurance wouldn't cover us because the operation wasn't under a contract. At first, I thought it wouldn't be a problem. Then I started searching for an insurance company that would cover our operation.

Time was up in Southern California, so we headed back to Eureka. The first thing I did was check the finances, and I was stunned. We had raised over $50,000, with more funds coming in every day. This venture had once been a pipe dream, but now it was real. I realized we were going to make it work. All I needed was to get the necessary insurance to load the ship.

I reached out to local insurance companies I was familiar with. Each one denied my request for the same reason as Stevedore's insurance company. I also contacted international firms but received the same response. My heart sank. This one issue could ruin the project and undo all our hard work.

I wasn't sure what to try next. I lay in bed at night feeling so frustrated that I couldn't sleep. At three in the morning, it suddenly hit me: the only reason I needed insurance was for the forklift and a few loading straps. Why couldn't I rent a forklift from a local rental yard? If needed, I would buy the loading straps. Would this approach work?

Excited, I called Jose the next morning and told him about my problem. I asked if I could rent a forklift to load the ship. He said he didn't see why not. I was elated; I felt like I had won the Super Bowl all by myself!

I called Castle and Cooke and told them we were ready to move forward with the project. Requirements had been met, and we had the funding to proceed.

They ordered the ship and would notify me in a few days when it was expected to arrive. To avoid excessive port fees, the materials needed to be at the dock on the day the ship arrived. We had to get them loaded the same day so the ship could depart as soon as possible. I agreed, promising that we would be there.

I ordered the materials from the lumber yard. Now I needed a place to store them. I worked for McMurray and Sons Roofing Company, doing carpentry work for them. McMurray and Sons was the fifth-largest roofing company in the state of California. They had a huge yard, large enough to store all the materials.

Dave McMurray, the owner, had donated to my previous projects and was very supportive of the Latin American venture. He had traveled to Guatemala with work teams and said it changed his life. He knew Bob Trolese personally and tracked the progress of the housing project. Not only did Dave store the materials, but he also arranged shipping from Eureka to the docks in Long Beach.

The final obstacle was overcome. Nothing can hold us back now.

The moment had arrived to pull the trigger. Everything was in place, with funding still coming through. As I waited for the call from Castle and Cooke, I realized I needed partners for the trip to Nicaragua. I had two other men with construction experience joining me: Milton Marsh and Gary Salyer.

Milton was a skilled carpenter and a veteran of World War II. He served with the Marines on Okinawa as a Navy corpsman. He didn't talk about it much, but I could tell that terrible battle still haunted him. When I invited Milton on this trip, he jumped at the chance, as if it would bring some closure to his life. He died suddenly just after we returned.

Gary, a roofer from Redding, California, had a rough appearance but a kind heart. He recently went through a divorce from his wife of over twenty years and was feeling its effects. His ex-wife, Dixie, wanted out of the marriage and took him to the cleaners. This upset him. He was living in his parents' travel trailer next to their house. When I asked him to come, he thought the trip would do him some good.

I asked Castle and Cooke what it would take for the three of us to travel to Nicaragua by ship. They said it was permitted, but we needed to pay $100 per person for food.

"Wow!" I thought. "We get to take this cruise down the coast of Latin America for only a hundred dollars. How cool is that!"

Voyage to Nicaragua

Standing at the dock early in the morning, four 40-foot trailer loads of building materials waited to be loaded onto the ship. Lucille, the kids, and my mother-in-law were with me. I didn't want them to miss this event. The boys were excited to watch a big ship come in and tie up. To prevent the longshoremen from getting hungry, I had hired a caterer to bring sandwich makings and drinks.

Longshoremen arrived as Gary was driving the forklift from the rental yard. Looking up, I saw the bow of a white ship slowly being nudged by tugs, rounding the corner of the dock and coming fully into view.

Tropical Sun was an older ship with a superstructure amidships, cargo hatches, and cranes fore and aft. Left over from a romantic era in shipping, she had staterooms to carry one hundred passengers. It had been possible to buy a berth and travel to distant ports for fun and adventure. Following the rise of the jet plane, this type of travel largely disappeared. Most of these ships were sold for scrap metal.

Fortunately for us, the Tropical Sun still managed to get us to Nicaragua.

Once it was secured at the dock, the longshoremen headed straight to work. Their first task was to go to the fenced-in area where the Stevedore Company kept its equipment and unlock the gate.

They gathered the necessary gear to load the ship, fired up their forklifts, and got busy. I tried to tell them we weren't supposed to use that equipment, but they ignored me and kept going. I thought, This is going to be interesting if anybody from the stevedore company shows up.

But I didn't say anything. The forklift we hired to do the job stayed in place until the ship was loaded. It was never used.

The captain came down and invited us aboard. He showed us the main salon, where snacks were laid out on the table. The officers were Norwegian, and the crew was Filipino. My mother-in-law was in her element, chatting up the young, tanned, good-looking Norwegians. The captain was a portly, seasoned seaman with some miles on him—his demeanor made us feel welcome.

I looked out the porthole at the last of our materials being loaded. I felt this would be a nice ending. However, we still had to travel to Nicaragua and build one hundred houses.

It was time to cast off and head south. My family was on the dock to watch us leave. Gary returned from returning the forklift. With everything stowed in our cabins, we thanked the longshoremen as they departed. While tidying up where the caterers had set up, there stood the man from the stevedore company. He smiled and asked how the loading went. I told him, "No problems." He had heard we used his equipment. I sheepishly shrugged my shoulders. He shook my hand and wished us luck.

I kissed my family goodbye, expecting to see them in about a month, and headed up the gangway. The ship's crew cast off the lines, the tugs waited, and we set sail.

A bright red sunset lit up the sky as we sailed out of Long Beach Harbor. Dinner was served in the salon— raw fish in a special Norwegian white sauce. Two Filipino stewards dressed in white attended to all our needs.

Officers dressed for dinner were present, except for those on watch. Engaging in small talk and getting to know each other made the three of us feel like honored guests. This was a special moment, and I wanted to cherish it. It was a once-in-a-lifetime experience to be on an old tramp steamer heading south, possibly to rewrite history.

After dinner, we retreated to our rooms. Amid all the excitement of loading the ship, I took a shower and collapsed into bed, falling asleep almost instantly to the hum of the ship's engines. But I woke up during the night, being tossed around my bunk. All was quiet; the engines had stopped.

The vessel was riding a swell, rocking heavily. I lay there, wondering what was happening, too tired to get up and investigate.

The morning sun shone through the porthole. We were moving again. A knock on the door from the steward signaled it was time for breakfast: eggs, bacon, sausage, potatoes, fruit, juice, coffee, and sweet rolls. I was told that one of the engines had failed during the night. There's no need to worry; we can continue just fine with one engine. It slowed us down, but we expect to arrive in Corinto in six days.

I spent most of my time on the bridge, enjoying the incredible view and gaining firsthand knowledge of the weather conditions. On the third day out, we were passing Cabo San Lucas at the southern tip of Baja California. The weather reports warned us of a storm brewing in the Bite.

The Bite is located on the border between Mexico and Guatemala. A strong northeast wind from the Caribbean blows across Central America, heating up. When it reaches the Pacific side, it becomes fierce. Sailing into sixty-mile-per-hour winds, there was no way to predict how high the seas would rise.

As we neared the storm, we felt the sea begin to change. The ship rose and fell with the swells. The wind picked up, and soon we were right in the middle of the storm. On the bridge, I held on for dear life as the bow of the ship buried itself in the oncoming waves. Water and spray towered over the superstructure as we battled thirty-foot waves for what felt like hours.

Late that afternoon, I noticed a change. Subtle at first, I realized the storm had passed. With the sun setting, we sailed on calm seas, heading closer to our destination.

From the deck the next morning, we could see the Nicaraguan coast—a dark blur on the horizon. The blur grew clearer, and soon we identified tropical trees. The ship's radioman was talking with the port captain, and the harbor pilot was on his way to meet us.

I anxiously wondered what would happen when we arrived. I knew the Sandinista government was paranoid about non-communist vessels entering their ports and inspecting them for contraband.

My primary concern was the $10,000 in cash I was carrying to cover the project expenses. I placed the money in a manila envelope and tucked it into my pants under my shirt for safekeeping.

With the harbor pilot boat alongside, it wouldn't be long before our voyage was over. The captain asked us to hand over our passports so he could clear us through Nicaraguan customs. The harbor pilot took control of our ship and slowly guided us into Corinto Bay alongside the wharf to moor the vessel.

Longshoremen waited to unload the ship while we finished customs. Next to them stood twenty soldiers with AK-47s, which created a menacing scene that made us feel uneasy. Bob and Alfred waved from the dock, and I was happy to see them.

The ship was secured, and the gangway was lowered onto the dock. The first people to board were the soldiers with their loaded AK-47s. They were all business, no smiles, as they hurried to take positions around the ship. I wasn't prepared for this kind of treatment, especially since we were giving them a gift of one hundred new homes.

Ordered to stay in the salon, the soldiers searched the entire ship. I'm not sure what they were looking for, maybe mercenaries, thinking we would foment a counterrevolution. You could have cut the tension with a knife; it was so thick. With ten thousand dollars tucked in my pants, I was nervous as hell, and it probably showed on my face. The last time I dealt with communists was in Vietnam.

The captain broke the ice by yelling, "Hey Bob, watch this!"

He grabbed three oranges off the table and started juggling with a smile on his face.

"What do you think, Bob? Could I make it to the circus?"

It worked, and I started to laugh. Even the guards cracked smiles.

While the guards inspected the ship, a customs official came aboard to process our passports and visas. A military officer told us to start unloading the ship as Bob and Alfred entered the salon. Man, was I glad to see them! Hugs all around—we had made it to Nicaragua with a ship full of building materials. It seemed unreal.

Bob and Alfred took over their part, greatly easing my load. Handing the manila folder to Alfred, I felt much lighter as I looked forward to unloading the ship.

Corinto had a railhead with a train of ten flatcars waiting to transfer our cargo to Managua. It would take all night to finish the freight transfer. Official procedures needed to be completed to clear us through customs.

We showed the bill of lading to the customs official, a young Black man named Rodolfo. He spoke English and was well-versed in his job. In private, he told us that when the Sandinistas took control, he had tried to leave the country for the United States, where he had family. The government quickly told him it wouldn't be allowed; he was the only one at the port who knew what he was doing. Captured by the new government, it was clear he wasn't happy with how things had changed.

Gratefully acknowledging our assistance on behalf of his people, he expedited the process. Official paperwork was completed, and the longshoremen began unloading the cargo.

Gary, Milton, and I spent our last night on the ship while unloading was still happening. After dinner, I went to bed. Almost asleep, Gary knocked on my door. Excited, he said they were destroying the crate that held the paint. Several of the cans had burst open, and paint was spilling everywhere. He had tried telling the longshoremen to stop so he could save as much paint as possible, but they ignored him because he didn't speak Spanish. He came to get me so I could try to communicate with them.

My Spanish wasn't perfect, but I got dressed and followed Gary down to the hold. Paint was splattered everywhere. The crate was wrecked, and the workers gathered the good cans, placing them on wooden pallets. There was nothing I could do but let them proceed.

Too hyped to fall back asleep, I spent the rest of the night on deck with Gary, watching them unload the ship. When the sun rose, tired and bleary-eyed from lack of sleep, I stumbled around, drinking as much coffee as I could hold.

Mid-morning, the ship was unloaded, and materials were loaded onto flat cars. The train would arrive in Managua in three days. I worried about leaving it behind, but the military assured us that it would be safe.

Armed guards will protect our valuable cargo.

It was time to leave. As we disembarked, we gathered our belongings and said farewell to the captain and crew. It was an emotional goodbye because we had grown close and formed lasting friendships. Sharing warm handshakes and goodbyes, we walked down the gangway one last time.

There was one last inspection before we left for Managua—of our personal belongings. As we entered the inspection station, we were told to open all our luggage. Once again, I was surprised they would subject us to this final hassle. The inspectors examined every item, taking a considerable amount of time.

Bob was growing increasingly frustrated. He had had enough. He stormed into the main office, slamming the door behind him. I couldn't hear what was being said, but through the window, I saw Bob yelling at the head customs official, waving his arms in the air. The official stood up from his chair and walked with Bob to where we were. He paused for a moment, watching the situation, then leaned over and spoke softly into the inspector's ear. We were told to repack our belongings; we were then free to leave.

In no time, we packed up and left. Bob and Alfred's van was ready. We threw our stuff in the back and climbed in with Alfred driving. On a beautiful, sunny tropical day, it wasn't long before I dozed off, missing sights along the way.

We arrived at several small houses surrounded by a concrete wall. The women had prepared a meal for us. We sat down to discuss our trip and the drama that accompanied it.

Waiting for the train gave us time to recover from our trip and adjust to our new surroundings. As night fell, we headed to our shelter. After a cold shower, I crawled into bed, knowing the most challenging part was behind me. I looked forward to moving on to the real task of building one hundred homes.

We woke up to the crowing of roosters and the barking of dogs. After a nice breakfast, the Creole boys stopped by for a visit. We got along well. By mid-afternoon, we grew restless and wanted to go out and check out the construction site.

The people receiving the houses were working at the site when we arrived. A young woman named Lesbia supervised the workers.

Bob and Alfred took us to one of the few remaining steakhouses after the war. We tasted Nicaraguan meat for the first time. The steakhouse was an open-air spot with a large, thatched roof. Tables were set on a terracotta floor surrounding an open barbecue pit, where smoke mingled with the aroma of large slabs of roasting meat. It was suggested that we order the Churrasco, a pound of beef cooked to perfection and topped with a sauce made from parsley and vinegar. It was delicious, and with a bowl of black bean soup, it became one of my favorite meals whenever I went out to dine.

We arrived at the work site the following morning and began setting out the lots, planning to install block foundations. We calculated the number of blocks needed and ordered them from a local vendor, along with sand and cement, for twenty units. Once each house was laid out, it was up to the community members to dig the footings. They went straight to work with picks and shovels. It was a proud moment to see the project in progress.

At the end of the day, the train arrived at the Managua rail station with the materials. Bob arranged trucks to deliver the materials to the work site. Leaving the Creole boys in charge of the digging, we headed to the train station. With Army guards protecting our cargo, we reached another milestone.

The project took on a life of its own. As the materials arrived, workers were digging footings, and masons laid the blocks. Since all the units were identical, we set up jigs and cut the lumber to the correct size. We built a large jig table with designated spots for each part of the wall and roof trusses. It was easy to position each piece in its place and nail it together.

Completed walls were carried by hand to the foundation and raised; the corners were nailed together. Milton took over and finished the work with his handpicked crew. Once the trusses were nailed in place, Gary and his crew applied the metal roofing. By the third day, everyone had been assigned their individual tasks.

Gary, Milton, and I took a step back and watched the entire project come together. We had reached our goal. After two weeks, it was time to head home. The Nicaraguans threw a party to say farewell. It was a bittersweet moment that would forever stay with us

Coming Home

Back in my living room, I sat on the couch, wondering what to do next. It was hard to believe it was over. Oddly, when I attended a church leadership meeting shortly afterward, little was said about the Nicaragua project. At the end of the meeting, someone asked about the progress of the housing project.

I said, "It all worked out well."

No more was said about it, which didn't bother me. I kept it to myself, Milton, and Gary.

Guatemala

Alfred and his family returned to Guatemala, where Verbo Ministries was launching a humanitarian project called "International Love Lift" to assist impoverished communities. Alfred was chosen to lead that project.

Once established in Guatemala, Alfred called and asked if I would serve as the representative in the United States. Assigned to payroll, my duties included raising funds and organizing work teams for proposed projects. I set up an office in Eureka and flew to Guatemala to meet with Alfred. One project involved establishing Christian schools throughout Guatemala City. Our task was to help revamp or build new facilities for these schools.

Retired Guatemalan General Efraín Ríos Montt became a follower of Verbo Ministries. He was asked to oversee the schools along with another friend, Dick Funnel. General Ríos Montt had previously served as the head of the Guatemalan Military Academy before retiring from the Army. Under his leadership, these schools became very successful and a popular choice for children seeking quality education. I had several opportunities to meet with General Ríos Montt. Thanks to our military backgrounds, we became friends and work partners.

The Military Coup

During this period, young captains in the Guatemalan Army organized a military coup. Led by Captain Muñoz, they toppled the corrupt Guatemalan government. The Army had been involved in a lengthy war with a revolutionary insurgency along the Mexican border. The captains bore the brunt of this fight and were uncertain if they were winning. They realized they had to earn the trust and support of the indigenous people to make progress. Many of them had received training from Ríos Montt while attending the military academy and believed he was an honest and upright man they could trust.

Aware of what Ríos Montt had accomplished in the Verbo system through his building of schools and other humanitarian efforts, they contacted him to lead the government. It was a tough decision. He asked the church leaders to gather for prayer and discussion before making any choices.

However, church leadership was concerned because Ríos Montt had been accused of genocide against thousands of indigenous people on the Mexican border. They couldn't support him if these allegations were factual.

I wasn't present at those meetings, but I learned what was happening through phone calls with Alfred. Ríos Montt claimed he never ordered any genocide and had evidence to convince the church leadership.

They decided to support him if he accepted the offer from these young captains. This became major international news, shining a spotlight not only on Ríos Montt but also on the entire Verbo ministry.

Media Attention

Because of my connections with Verbo Ministries, Gospel Outreach, and International Love Lift, I was tasked with handling numerous phone calls from international press representatives. I was out of my depth but did my best given the situation. I managed visits from roaming reporters trying to figure out how this Jesus People group in Eureka, California, could be linked to military coups in Latin America. Instead of accepting that it simply happened, they searched for some conspiracy.

After the dust settled, I was assigned to travel to Guatemala for a series of meetings. Ríos Montt wanted to keep the church leadership informed as part of his kitchen cabinet advisory group. I was considered part of that kitchen cabinet. Two of the church leaders, Francisco Bianchi and Álvaro Contreras, became his personal secretaries

The Border Conflict

One issue that arose was the conflict on the border. The genocide issue persisted as the war remained intense. Ríos Montt asked for suggestions.

Without thinking, I spoke and said I believed every man has a right to defend his family and community. We should arm these vulnerable groups so they can protect themselves and provide enough to feed their families until this ends.

The room went quiet. I sat there, wondering what I had said. Then, the meeting ended. Before we left, Ríos Montt asked Alfred and me to speak with him. He inquired whether we would be willing to fly out to several burned-out villages to see firsthand what was happening. We agreed.

Later that day, we received a phone call telling us to be at the airport on the military side at 8 AM. A helicopter would take us out to the villages. At eight the next morning, we were there, along with Jon Omey, my dentist from Eureka.

As we flew into the first village, it was heartbreaking to see the abandoned, charred remains of what had once been a lively community. Fields of corn and other crops that were left untended surrounded it. Someone did this. They set fire to this place. We suspected it was either a wayward Guatemalan military unit or a counter-revolutionary group trying to punish villagers for not joining the revolution. We didn't know who was responsible. But my experience in the Vietnam War taught me what happens to people caught in the middle of conflicts. I began to wonder what Ríos Montt had in mind for Alfred and me as we flew back to Guatemala City.

The helicopter touched down, and Alfred and I were invited to Captain Muñoz's house for dinner. I looked forward to spending time with him and his family and didn't want to miss it. We arrived on time and were warmly welcomed into their home, where his wife and two young boys were waiting.

Two other men joined us. I wasn't sure who they were. After introductions, we sat down to get acquainted. Our meal of typical Guatemalan cuisine was delicious, featuring black bean soup and a variety of desserts.

After the meal, Captain Muñoz's wife and her boys left the room, giving the men space to discuss the matters at hand. The two other men were Israeli military officers there to advise on training. I felt insecure, but I enjoyed being part of it.

Captain Muñoz expressed concern about the conflict on the border and inquired about how Alfred and I could assist by contacting those involved. Nothing was settled that night, but Alfred and I knew they relied on us to help resolve the issue.

Beans and Bullets

The next day, Alfred and I met with Ríos Montt and listened to his plan. He aimed to start a program called "Beans and Bullets." The plan involved arming vulnerable villagers so they could defend themselves, while ensuring they had sufficient supplies to support their families. That shocked me because I was the one who had introduced the idea at the meeting. He wanted our help with the food part of the program.

Alfred and I agreed to pull this off, but we needed something bigger than what we had. His idea was to create another, more neutral group. We established FUNDAPI, which stands for the Foundation for the Indigenous People. With FUNDAPI in place, we could attract a broader range of agencies willing to help.

Evangelical Attention

Because Ríos Montt was an evangelical Christian and the President of a Latin American country, it attracted attention from major Christian groups abroad. The first prominent evangelist to notice was Pat Robertson of the *700 Club*. Pat flew to Guatemala on his own initiative and secured an interview with Ríos Montt. He then flew back to Virginia and aired it the following day.

From then on, it seemed like every televangelist tried to join the program. Pat Robertson was a massive help throughout the entire episode. He assisted with finances and introduced us to other people who came to our support.

The Nabaj Mission

Our first project with FUNDAPI involved sending a dental team to the Ixil Triangle, a region affected by conflict. We organized a dental clinic in a small village called Nabaj. Jon Omey coordinated the dentists from the United States. We invited the Elliotts, who had lived in Nabaj as missionaries for thirty years. They had left because of the war. Another team member was an older German doctor who had married an Ixil Indian woman. He had established a clinic in Chichicastenango. To complete the team, an American well digger joined us. He also married an Indian woman and was familiar with the area. A film crew from the 700 Club came to document the event.

Alfred and I were supposed to escort the team by helicopter to Nabaj. We rented a small hotel for five days to host the team.

Alfred and I were scheduled to return the same day for a meeting with representatives from the U.S. State Department. This was an important meeting. They had approved $60 million in U.S. aid to the previous government, but the Carter administration delayed it because of human rights abuses. Ríos Montt wanted Alfred and me to attend the meeting to explain efforts to reduce further abuses.

The dental team gathered in Guatemala City, preparing to depart the next day. Two Army helicopters were on standby to carry us and our gear to Nabaj. Jon Omey brought three other dentists from Eureka. The dentists' wives stayed behind to go shopping.

That night, we met at the Presidential Palace for dinner with Ríos Montt and his wife. The next morning at the airport, we loaded the helicopters and took off, with the wives waving goodbye from the tarmac.

Under Fire in Nabaj

The heavily loaded choppers made the trip from the city to Nabaj. Flying over a 12,000-foot mountain range, which was the maximum altitude for the choppers, became tricky. As we approached the range, I felt nervous, not only for my own safety but also for the safety of the team.

The pilots squeezed through a gap in the mountains. On the other side, within view, sat the village of Nabaj tucked in a small valley.

Suddenly, as we were about to land on the town soccer field, we were caught in crossfire and ambushed by insurgents. The helicopters had M-60 machine guns mounted on each side. They touched down just long enough to disembark us, unload our gear, and then lifted off again to rejoin the fight.

A group of Guatemalan soldiers hurried to escort us into a building in the center of the town square. Across the street, a grand Catholic cathedral loomed tall. Bullets whizzed everywhere. I felt helpless. I knew I had to get our team out of there right away. There was no way I was going to let them stay in that danger. What would I tell their wives if something happened to them?

Adding to the chaos, after the shooting stopped, the helicopters returned to land, and the second chopper crashed and rolled over. What a mess this was becoming! The film crew saw an excellent opportunity to get good footage and rushed onto the football field, recording the entire event. The rest of us hurried down to help in any way we could.

The army rescued the crew from the helicopter that had flipped upside down. A couple was injured, but no one was killed.

I gathered the team by the fountain in front of the church. I was rushing to get them out of there as quickly as I could. They weren't staying.

The team held their own meeting and told me they wouldn't be leaving. They arrived for a mission and planned to finish it. It was an awkward moment. In the end, I gave in, with serious doubts.

With only one chopper, we couldn't leave anyway. At the hotel, I assisted them with getting settled. When the commander of the Army compound came to greet us, he was grateful that we had arrived and apologized for the shootout. He assured us we would be well protected during our stay.

To Guatemala City

It was late in the afternoon when another helicopter arrived to pick up Alfred and me. We had a meeting in the city to attend. We said goodbye to our team, boarded the aircraft, and headed back. Alfred mentioned he didn't feel good about the situation, but it was too late to change our minds. We decided not to tell the wives.

We got back just in time to rush to the meeting without having dinner. Two people from the State Department were there with a man named Harris Whitbeck. I noticed a Marine Corps tie clip on Harris and asked him if he was a Marine. He said he was, and I told him I was, too. I felt good about Harris Whitbeck.

The meeting was about the $60 million and how we could access it. We discovered it wouldn't be easy. We were told it would be best if Ríos Montt assembled a small delegation to go to Washington, D.C., for PR work with the authorities. That started a long process. I was so exhausted from the day's activities that most of the meeting went over my head. Additionally, I was worried about the team left in the field.

The next few days were busy with commitments and caring for the dentist's wives. I stayed alert for any news from Nabaj. I tried to get back there, but no flights were heading that way.

I noticed Harris was lingering even after the other two men left. I began to question where he fits into the overall picture. I never figured it out but assumed he was CIA—he was always nearby.

Mission Accomplished

The day arrived when the team was supposed to return. I drove to the airport to meet them. As the day went on, no one showed up. I found out that the weather had gotten worse, and they couldn't leave.

They arrived the next day with a story to tell. I felt relieved to see the chopper land on the tarmac. They stepped out with big smiles. It was apparent they were just as happy to be back as I was to see them. Gunfights had been raging in the streets of Nabaj at night while they hid inside their hotel, with its large wooden doors locked tight.

During the day, it was a different story. They treated hundreds of patients and extracted thousands of teeth. When residents from the nearby areas heard about the dental clinic, they risked crossing roving bands of insurgents and came to town. No one was turned away. The mission was a huge success—the start of a new era in the region.

The next step was for the delegation to travel to Washington. The delegation included Francisco Bianchi, the private secretary to Ríos Montt; Carlos Ramírez, the head pastor of the Verbo Church; Álvaro Contreras; and me.

We flew to Virginia Beach, Virginia. Carlos had a speaking engagement at the Rock Church. We met Pastor John Giménez and his wife Ann. Then, we went to the 700 Club to meet Pat Robertson and do an interview for his show. John Giménez came with us. After the show, he told Pat we were short on cash. Pat gave us $5,000 to help cover expenses.

John told us we needed to contact a guy named Bob Pettinger. Bob Pettinger worked for a Christian lobby group sponsored by Campus Crusade. He knew everyone in Washington, including the key figures in Christendom.

John contacted Pettinger on our behalf and requested a meeting. Pettinger lived outside Washington, D.C. and was willing to meet us the next day. We rented a car and drove up that night. During the drive, Carlos dropped a bombshell on us: he had received a call from the Verbo Church, and it seemed he was having an affair with one of the women there. She eventually came to the leadership and confessed her sins.

WHAM!!! That knocked the wind out of our sails. For the moment, we set it aside and stuck to our schedule. Once Eureka's leadership heard about Carlos's mistake, he was called back to Eureka. They decided he couldn't stay as head of Verbo until this issue was resolved. For now, he was out of the loop.

We met with Pettinger, and he agreed to support our cause. From then on, we quickly engaged in numerous activities. We met with congressmen, senators, cabinet members, and prominent leaders of churches of all sizes and denominations.

Pettinger arranged meetings with Ronald Reagan's kitchen cabinet. We had breakfast in Washington, D.C., lunch in Dallas, and dinner in Denver, then flew back to Washington for more meetings. Between working in the field in Guatemala and three additional trips to D.C., I was home for only seven days over the next four months.

Refugee Crisis and Relief Efforts

During the second trip to Nabaj with another dental team, the guerrillas released 3,000 Indians they had been holding captive. They couldn't feed them, so they sent them to Nabaj, where the missionaries were, recalling the Elliotts. They arrived one day like a large herd. Initially, we separated them into separate households. I was amazed at how the Ixil people accepted this inconvenience without a single complaint.

The Army left a lot of timber along the sides of the roads. They cut down trees fifty meters on each side to protect themselves from ambushes. With a sawmill, we could process this timber and use it to build shelters for newly arrived refugees.

I returned to the United States and purchased a sawmill. While there, I received donations from Calvary Chapel for seven thousand pieces of laminated roofing for these shelters.

The Mercy Ships organization in Long Beach was getting ready for a Latin American outreach. I asked them if they could bring the sawmill and roofing materials to Guatemala. I took Don Stevens, the head of Mercy Ships, out to lunch. He was well informed about what was happening.

Guatemala was their first stop. The sawmill and roofing materials were delivered to the dock, and I watched as they were loaded. Then I traveled to Guatemala to wait for their arrival. This took less than three weeks.

While I was away, Alfred discovered a USAID reforestation grant available for the Ixil area. He applied for and received the funding. With this grant, we helped refugees rebuild their lives and settle into their new communities.

Once the Mercy Ship arrived, we delivered the sawmill and roofing to Nabaj, assembled the mill, and began cutting wood. It wasn't long before the shelters were built and families moved in. With this effort, peace settled in the region, and daily life was established. It wasn't easy; it was simply hard work.

Final Attempt for U.S. Aid

We made another trip to Washington to secure the $60 million. We needed to persuade the appropriations committee of our good intentions. During our journey, we met Dr. Richard McCormick, who served as the Undersecretary of Finance for Latin American Affairs at the U.S. Department of State. He scheduled several meetings with key members of Congress to pressure the Appropriations Committee into releasing the funds.

In the field, sick with dysentery, I was told a chopper was coming to pick me up. I went straight to the airport for a flight to Washington for an important meeting with the Appropriations Committee. My clothes were packed. When I landed at the airport, I boarded the flight to D.C. immediately. I was sick and hadn't showered for a week. I arrived in D.C. just in time to go to the hotel, take a shower, and change into my brown suit.

Entering the State Department building, I thought I needed to pass gas, but I ended up soiling myself. I went to the restroom to clean up as best I could, then attended the meeting Dr. McCormick had arranged with a young staffer named Holly. I told her what was happening in Nabaj and how the situation was changing. She asked if the Guatemalan Army was in the village. I confirmed yes. She shook her head, closed her notebook, and left the room.

We didn't receive the money.

The Pope and Ríos Montt

The Pope visited Guatemala. Ríos Montt was at the airport to welcome him. This was an unusual event. Ríos Montt had been a Catholic before converting to the Verbo Church, becoming evangelical.

According to Church tradition, Ríos Montt was expected to kiss the Pope's ring. People watched as Ríos Montt shook his hand instead. That marked the beginning of the end.

Four men in a bar had murdered four people and raped several women. They were caught, tried, and sentenced to death. The Vatican asked Ríos Montt to revoke the death penalty, and he sentenced them to life in prison. Under Guatemalan law, the verdict must be carried out within 48 hours. Ríos Montt had to choose between honoring the Church's request and following Guatemalan law. He chose Guatemalan law. Things fell apart.

The U.S. government wanted Ríos Montt to honor the Catholics but heard that he was supposed to follow Guatemalan law and execute the offenders. I was in Eureka working in the same office as Carlos Ramírez, who was serving time for his infidelity. Nobody told Ríos Montt about Carlos's indiscretion. They didn't want to burden him.

Admiral Mittendorf, the U.S. Ambassador to the Organization of American States (OAS), called me to ask for Francisco Bianchi's phone number. He wanted to persuade Ríos Montt to reconsider the execution.

Carlos was yelling at me not to give him the number. I gave the number, but Mittendorf was unsuccessful, and the execution continued.

Carlos thought I was trying to take over his position at the Verbo Church. I told him that was crazy. I was trying to do a good job. Carlos, officially the head of Verbo, asked me to resign.

The Fall of Ríos Montt

The U.S. Navy sent the USS Ranger to the coast of Guatemala and requested that Ríos Montt visit the ship. While on the Ranger, a countercoup took place, and a colonel assumed control of the government. Upon his return, Ríos Montt was placed under house arrest.

Along with Harris Whitbeck, many in the Army wanted to retake the presidency through violence, but Ríos Montt told them to stand down. He didn't want any bloodshed. I later heard that the U.S. authorized the coup, with the condition that Ríos Montt not be harmed.

I believe Carlos was trying to control Ríos Montt, and the rivalry between Catholics and Evangelicals caused the downfall of the government. Carlos wanted to be the spiritual leader of Guatemala, too naive to understand the implications.

The Catholics won.

First Marriage Breakup and a Broken Neck

My involvement with the Guatemalan government ultimately hurt my relationship with Lucille, although I didn't realize it at the time.

After Carlos let me go, I felt a little down. Gospel Outreach was changing as people got older and moved away from the ministry's strict rules. George and Marie were among the first to leave, moving to Redding, California, where George was trying to start his own advertising paper. Since they were close friends, they asked Lucille and me to go with them. It was an exciting idea, but I needed to work first.

Bob Perry, a wealthy businessman from Redding, owned a sawmill and a company that developed small hydro projects in the Sierra Nevada foothills. I knew Bob well—he had donated thousands of dollars to many of my projects and traveled with me on numerous trips to Latin America. When he heard I was considering moving to his area, he offered me a job at his company building spec houses.

I left my family in Eureka until I was established, returning home on weekends. At first, things went smoothly. We found a suitable property for a spec house, and Bob purchased it. We set up a division of his company using my contractor's license, which we named Northwestern Construction. His friend drew up plans and designed a small house to fit the lot.

After obtaining the necessary permits and starting construction, Bob's sons became my helpers. Bob owned a large house with two basement rooms where I stayed.

Then I got the news.

One Thursday night, while having dinner with Bob's family, the phone rang. It was Lucille asking to speak to me. I answered the call, thinking she wanted to check on how things were going. She asked about my work, and I gave her an update on our progress. Then she told me she had filed papers for divorce.

At first, I thought she was joking. I quickly realized she was serious. Shocked, I stayed in Redding for a week before heading home to figure out what to do. I could tell I wasn't welcome in my own house.

I returned to Redding to finish the house. Once it was livable enough, I moved in and slept on the floor. It was horrible and very depressing.

When my boys stayed with me for a week, I realized I needed to go back to Eureka and start picking up the pieces.

After completing the house, I thank Bob for everything he did for me and then head back to the coast.

The only place I knew to go was back to Lighthouse Ranch. I moved in with a friend until I could get my footing and found work with another friend, Roger Smith, who was building a large apartment complex in Fortuna. When the framing contractor on the job got a nail in his eye and couldn't work, Roger asked if I would take over and run the project.

During that period, I started experiencing problems on my left side. It weakened gradually until I could barely lift my arm. I saw a neurologist who suspected ALS—Lou Gehrig's disease, a fatal, incurable brain disorder. After tests ruled out ALS, he referred me to physical therapy. It seemed to help, but I continued to face major challenges.

That's when Jim Durkin contacted me. The ranch faced serious issues and needed a new septic system. The county had been warning them for years that the current system was inadequate and required upgrading to support the residents. If nothing was done, they would shut down the ranch. He asked me to handle this project. I would be paid for the work, but I had to raise both the funds for the project and my salary. I wasn't feeling well, but I agreed to take on the project anyway.

I organized a fundraising effort with local businesses and developed the new system in collaboration with a ranch resident. This experienced electrical engineer, who had burned out on life, felt the ranch was the right place for him.

The local community admired Lighthouse Ranch. Local businesses contributed generously, and funding and materials for the project arrived quickly. After four months, the project was finished.

Having finished the project, I expected to get paid. However, the leadership informed me that they wouldn't be paying me. They thought I should do it "unto the Lord." That hurt my feelings, but I shrugged it off and moved on.

Physically, I was getting worse, constantly losing strength. One day, while building a garage for a friend, I woke up to find it extremely hard to get out of bed. Every time I tried to stand up, I would fall to the floor and struggle to get back on my feet. I didn't understand what was happening; I thought I was losing my mind.

Struggling to get dressed, I went to my truck, stumbling like a drunk. It took all I had to climb into the cab. When I arrived at the job site, I attempted to exit and fell to the ground. I couldn't get up. My friend called an ambulance, and I was taken to the hospital.

After a myelogram, the doctor told me I had broken my neck, specifically the seventh cervical vertebra. He performed a cervical laminectomy, and I was out of work for nearly a year.

A Place To Stay

Recovery was difficult. I applied for disability benefits, most of which went toward paying child support. I had nowhere to live and depended on friends for shelter and help. It's good to have friends.

After a couple of months, I was able to move around but couldn't return to my usual job. I started looking in the help-wanted section of the local paper for simple work I could do while recovering.

I found an ad for Rainbow Mini Storage, seeking a watchman and a light maintenance worker. The job included a one-bedroom apartment above one of the units. I had built those mini storage units years earlier and knew the owner, Ron Harris. I tore out the ad and went to his office. I hadn't seen Ron in a long time, and he was happy to see me.

He was shocked when I shared my medical and financial struggles and mentioned I was going through a divorce. Ron asked if there was anything he could do to help. I took out the ad, placed it on his desk, and told him I was applying for the job. He didn't hesitate and offered me the position immediately.

This marked the beginning of a significant turnaround. Ron took me to the site, showed me the apartment, and told me I could move in right away. The unit included a washer and dryer, along with a beautiful view of Humboldt Bay. I felt like I was back in the game, confident that everything would work out. My divorce was finalized, and I decided I would never marry again.

A New Career

While working at Rainbow Mini Storage, I was visited by Rob Bodie. Rob was involved with the Humboldt County Schools through the Regional Occupation Program, where he taught building trades at a local high school.

Rob told me about an opening for a building trades instructor at Fortuna High School and recommended I apply. I applied and secured the position. The best part was I could complete my teaching credential studies while working in the program. The position was fantastic, with summers off, paid, plus benefits.

After his retirement, Rob developed Alzheimer's, went into his backyard, and hanged himself.

One requirement was that thirty percent of the students needed to be employed in the building trades by the end of the year. The students in the class were non-academic; some were rough kids who had no plans for further education. The class provided them with the opportunity to explore the trades.

To introduce students to local contractors and tradespeople, I created an advisory board of ten contractors. Each class lasted two hours, and after two weeks of construction orientation, I would place some of my students with these contractors to gain real construction experience and potentially secure jobs by the end of the school year.

In this new career, I got off to a rough start. I didn't join the teachers' union because the class was part of the Regional Occupation Program, and membership wasn't required. I didn't want to bother with it since I was unaware of educational politics. If you weren't in the union, you were blacklisted.

My second mistake was implementing a discipline system: if one of my students was unruly or arrived late to class, they had to do push-ups. The number depended on the severity of the infraction. Being late for class earned twenty-five push-ups, while mouthing off in class could result in up to one hundred. I found that not only did parents appreciate the discipline, but the students, especially those who were troublemakers, did as well. However, the other teachers didn't appreciate it and wanted to report me for child abuse.

I quickly established a reputation with the faculty, but I didn't let it bother me. It was my class, and I was going to run it the way I believed was best. It's a dog-eat-dog world outside the classroom, and I felt my students might as well get used to it.

The first lecture I gave explained how God uniquely designed humans to be carpenters. I held up my hands and asked them to look at my fingers. I wrapped my hand around a hammer, demonstrating God's unique design. With my other hand, I picked up a nail and drove it into two pieces of wood, building a structure. Using a Skill saw, I cut another piece of wood and added it to the structure. They understood the message. They are capable of great things.

The first two weeks concentrated on tool safety training, including how to swing a hammer, use a skill saw, and operate other essential tools for success in the marketplace. We also covered blueprint reading, construction economics, and proper workplace attitudes.

Along with assigning students to work with contractors, the school administration had several projects they wanted our class to complete. The first was building covered bus stops so students waiting for pickup would be protected from rain. It was a good starting point. Our next project was enclosing the underside of the football bleachers for storage. It took two weeks to complete the project, and my students were proud of their first accomplishments.

School administrators, genuinely impressed, asked us to double the size of the snack bar. The class was gaining a reputation, and more people wanted to enroll.

Fridays were always pizza days. We would gather in the classroom to discuss how things went and assess our progress. Students learned much more by working on real-world construction projects than through classroom lessons. Contractors often bought pizza for the class as a gesture of appreciation, which sometimes got me into trouble for "taking bribes." Despite that, the class was a huge success.

This was the Reagan era, and Nancy Reagan was campaigning with her "Just Say No" anti-drug message. Humboldt County, where we lived, was the center of the marijuana-growing region, and most of my students smoked weed. Being a former drug user myself, I understood.

At one of my contractor board meetings, the discussion turned to the dangers of drug use destroying young people's minds. One member suggested offering cash rewards to my students to expose drug dealers. I mentioned this to my class, and it became so quiet you could hear a pin drop, as sad expressions filled the students' faces.

Two days later, after class, I was reviewing the next day's curriculum when one of my students approached me.

Very nervously, he said, "Mr. Means, you know what you said about exposing a drug dealer?"

My first thought was, how brave this kid is to go out on a limb and expose a drug dealer.

I was quickly corrected when he told me they got their drugs from their parents and couldn't turn in their own families.

I let the topic go and never mentioned it again.

Shane was a big kid with a talent for construction. He understood what we did quickly and loved working. He would have been the top student, except he was a constant bully, intimidating his classmates.

While I was lecturing about placing rebar in concrete footings, I noticed Shane flick another student's ear out of the corner of my eye. Having had enough of his antics, I stopped the lecture and told my students to leave the classroom—except for Shane.

They sat there in shock until I yelled louder, with an angry look on my face: "I WANT EVERYONE OUT OF THIS CLASSROOM RIGHT NOW, EXCEPT SHANE! AND THE LAST PERSON OUT, LOCK THE DOOR!"

There was a frantic rush toward the exit.

With Shane sitting there, I slowly moved a chair and sat down directly in front of him, gazing him in the eyes. I said, "You think you're pretty tough, don't you, Shane?"

Squirming, he replied, "Yeah."

I continued, "You're eighteen, aren't you? That means if we met behind the Ag Shop and fought it out, I couldn't go to jail for child abuse, could I?"

I guess not.

Making eye contact, expressionless, I asked, "You know the first thing I'm going to do to you?"

"No."

"I'm going to suck the eyeball out of your skull!"

No more issues from Shane.

I had an idea to take my class to Mexico to work on an orphanage 120 miles south of the border. The trip would happen near the end of the school year, offering an international cultural experience. Fortuna was a small town, and most of my students had never seen much of life outside that area.

I contacted the people running the orphanage to see if they needed our help. They were very open to us taking on many construction projects they required. The orphanage was twenty miles from the nearest town and had to be self-sufficient.

They needed housing for their staff. Volunteers came every year to help with the orphans, but there was no available housing for them. They wanted to lay the foundations for four small dwellings to accommodate married volunteer couples. Since they lacked the funds for this project, they asked if we could raise money for the materials. Having faced this problem before, we would do our best. Permission was required from the school board to make the trip.

This wasn't just about sending letters and gaining support. Taking eager students thirteen hundred miles away from home, into Mexico, involved navigating school and county regulations, as well as liability concerns. Was it even feasible?

Sharon Omey was a school board member and had participated in many mission trips. I told her about the project. She liked the idea and mentioned it at the next board meeting.

I waited for the meeting results, thinking that transportation and materials would also be significant issues. The local Rotary Club was well-known for its assistance with projects of this kind. Would they rent a van or two and cover the gas expenses?

Where would the funding come from for the trip and the materials needed to complete the project? Fortuna is in the heart of Redwood Country, and many of the students' parents worked for the Pacific Lumber Company. Would they provide a unit of 2x6 redwood?

A picnic table factory would give my students something to do on rainy days in my shop. Selling tables would cover the cost of materials.

Sharon called with good news: the board approved the trip, but they need a liability release from the parents of students under eighteen.

When I requested transportation assistance from the Rotary Club, they approved.

Pacific Lumber donated the 2x6 redwood unit for the picnic tables and even delivered it to our work site in their truck.

We were about to go to Mexico!

Setting up the picnic table factory was enjoyable. We built jigs similar to those used on the Nicaraguan housing project. Teams were organized for each part of the manufacturing process. The first team cut pieces to length for the tabletops, seats, and legs. The next team drilled holes in the wood for assembly.

Other teams assembled the tops, seats, crosspieces, and legs, then finished by tightening the final bolts.

The students began building these tables, competing to outdo each other. Every two hours, five tables were completed.

We had materials for fifty tables, each costing $50, totaling $2,500—more than enough to cover expenses. Requests for tables came in before they were finished, and we sold them all.

The departure date was set for mid-May. The students grew more excited as the time approached.

The day of departure arrived with two vans in the work area. Students came with their parents to see them off. We loaded the vans, waved goodbye, and headed south—an exciting moment for their first adventure.

Halfway through California, we found a campsite, and after stopping at Taco Bell for dinner, we settled in for the night. Some students stayed up late talking and carrying on as teenagers do.

At first light, we were up and ready to hit the road. Several students hadn't slept and quickly drifted off as soon as we started moving. We crossed into Tijuana, Mexico, at midday. I headed for an old surf spot I knew, which had a campground on the beach and a small cantina.

Just before dark, we set up camp on the beach. The drinking age in Mexico was eighteen, and I was told I couldn't stop them from going to the cantina. It wasn't long before most of them were completely drunk. The rest of the night was wild, as I tried to keep an eye on them and keep them out of trouble. It wasn't easy.

Getting everyone up and ready the next morning was tough. Some were so hungover they couldn't get out of bed, so we helped them up and carried them into the vans. We stopped in Ensenada for breakfast at a local restaurant I had visited many times before. Those who were too hungover stayed in the vans to sleep it off. Many students loaded up on bottle rockets before we hit the road again. In an hour, we would arrive.

While going through San Vicente, a small village, one of the students shouted, "Hey, look! That guy has a gun!" People started running, ducking, and dodging bullets right in front of us. My students thought it was the coolest thing they had ever seen. I sped up and got out of there.

The staff at the orphanage greeted us upon our arrival and directed us to a dormitory where we would spend the night. The dorm included kitchen facilities. We stopped in San Diego before crossing into Mexico and bought food to last us during our five-day stay. A friend had joined us on the trip to help with cooking.

We received a tour of the premises and the site where we planned to build three units. The orphanage was located a few miles off the main road in a large valley with rolling hills to the west and east. A road heading west from the orphanage led to the Pacific Ocean ten miles away. We took advantage of this later in the week.

Once we settled in, we ate lunch, grabbed picks and shovels, and began digging the footings for the units. The staff had already purchased the necessary materials to finish the project. By the end of the afternoon, we completed the footings, set the forms, and started mixing concrete for the first foundation.

We worked hard, ate well, and slept soundly all week. In the middle of the week, we took the afternoon off and went to the beach.

The beach was shrouded in thick fog. As we went along, we passed by miles of tall dunes. We had fun riding the dunes on pieces of plywood that others had left behind.

By the end of the week, we had completed our project, which involved roughing in underground plumbing and pouring the footings and slabs. All concrete was mixed by hand.

The night before we left, the staff and orphans threw a farewell party for us with hot dogs, hamburgers, drinks, and dessert. We had a good time but were ready to go home.

I had promised the students a trip to Disneyland as a reward for their hard work. Inside the park, they dispersed, promising to meet at the same spot at five o'clock. When five o'clock came, I did a head count and hadn't lost anyone. Two days later, we returned to Fortuna, hailed as heroes. The foundation was laid for future trips.

Chris was a cocky kid I found hard to handle. He knew exactly when to back off before I would attack. After the Mexico trip, we had a couple of weeks before break and built a mini golf course outside the classroom for tournaments. Chris liked to watch but didn't want to play.

I said, "Hey Chris, you're next to tee off."

His answer, "Blow me", got a giggle from the other students.

I pointed my finger at him and said, "I'm going to remember that."

The following year, I checked the roster and noticed Chris's name. I went to the vice principal and asked him to remove Chris from the list—I didn't want him in my class. No problem.

I received a call from Chris's angry mother, yelling at me and asking why I took Chris off the list when it was his favorite class.

I told her, "Ma'am, your son told me to suck his dick, and that offended me. I'm not having him in my class."

She shyly replied, "Oh."

That was the last time I heard about it.

Jesse was a tough case—his straight hair reached his shoulders, and he always wore black pants, AC/DC T-shirts, and black boots. His family had a long history as lumber mill workers, expecting him to follow their tradition. After we returned from Mexico, he came to me holding an essay he had written about the trip for his English class. There was an A+ in the top right corner, marked with a red pencil. He thanked me and said the trip had opened his eyes.

He didn't want to work in the mill but wanted to become a journalist. I said that was a good idea.

Another Switchback

Working with the school system had its highs and lows. After the trip to Mexico, I was blacklisted by the other faculty members. They were furious. I had done something unusual that reflected poorly on them. The woodshop teacher even went so far as to curse me out in front of the entire school during an assembly.

The agriculture teacher spread rumors that I was financially benefiting from my students' work for contractors. I was stunned when I was called to the administrator's office to address this accusation.

I discovered that the agriculture teacher started this rumor. I marched straight to his classroom to confront him. I asked where he got the information and why he didn't come to me first. He didn't really have an answer but said he needed to protect the students. I realized I'd have to watch my back.

The upside was that, by the end of the year, sixty percent of my students were hired into the workforce, and entire classes were scheduled for the following year. The other upside was that I received three months of paid leave during the summer.

That summer, a Christian relief organization asked me to lead a construction team to Nicaragua to work on the San Carlos orphanage outside of Managua. The team was already assembled, and I was eager to take on the project.

We arrived in Nicaragua and took a bus to the orphanage, where we saw a medical team from England running clinics with the orphans. The team included a young doctor and three nurses. We joined them, staying in the same guesthouse.

Every morning, I wake up before anyone else to make coffee and enjoy a couple of chocolate cookies. Juliet, one of the nurses, does the same but with tea.

Getting there before her, I developed the habit of boiling her water. She appreciated it but wouldn't let me make her tea — it had to be done just right. We sat at a small wooden table, having our morning chat. I asked why, at 41, she hadn't married. She said she'd never met the right man and figured that at her age, she was out of the competition

Explaining Juliet

Our Wedding

Juliet was a well-spoken English lady from an aristocratic family. I was attracted to her proper English accent and mannerisms.

Once I learned about her background in England, the best song I can think of to describe my relationship with Juliet is "If I Were a Carpenter and You Were a Lady."

To understand Juliet, it's essential to know her background. Her full name was Juliet Evelyn Mary Deedes, and she was born in the village of Aldington, Kent County, Southeast England, on October 22, 1948.

The Deedes surname is believed to have originated from William the Conqueror, who defeated Harold, King of the Anglo-Saxons, at the Battle of Hastings in 1066.

Over generations, the Deedes family accumulated large tracts of land in Kent County. Saltwood Castle served as their primary residence. The Deedes lived in and cared for the castle until 1925, when declining family finances made it impossible for them to continue.

A few generations before Juliet, most of the Deedes men were titled aristocratic military leaders.

Wyndham, her great-uncle, briefly served in South Africa during the Boer War. It was during World War I in Palestine, under General Allenby's command with T. E. Lawrence (also known as Lawrence of Arabia), that he made his mark in history.

Wyndham retired from the British Army as a Brigadier General, receiving Britain's highest honor, "The Victoria Cross." After his military service, he spent the rest of his life helping the poor and oppressed in the London suburbs.

In his later years, with his health failing, he retired to a small house by the shore in the Cinque Ports village of Hythe. When he died in 1956, he left his estate to Juliet's father, who then distributed it to his children. With Uncle Wyndham's inheritance, Juliet bought 95 North Road, a house on a hill overlooking St. Leonard's Church in Hythe. It had a side chapel for the Deedes family. On a clear day, you could see the shores of France from there.

T. E. Lawrence was well acquainted with the Deedes family, including Juliet's father. I remember him saying, "Lawrence was an odd fellow."

Like many aristocratic families in England, they shared a strong sense of duty and service to the nation. The Deedes were no different; their family crest motto read, "Deeds not words."

Calling members of the Deedes Family eccentric is an understatement.

Juliet's father, Bill Deedes, began his journalism career with the Morning Post in the 1920s. His first overseas assignment was covering the war in Abyssinia. There, he met the well-known correspondent Evelyn Waugh, who wrote a book about Bill's misadventures on the war front, titled "Scoop."

Before World War II, Bill lived with his uncle Wyndham in Bethnal Green to further his journalism career. When the war began, like other men in his family, he commissioned as a 2nd Lieutenant in the Territorial Battalion of the King's Royal Rifle Corps. During the Normandy landing, he was a Major with the 8th Armored Brigade.

During Operation "Market Garden," his unit was part of the 30th Corps, tasked with capturing and holding the bridges on the road to Arnhem, Holland. Once successful, he was to join up with the famous John Frost and the "First Paras" to defend the city. They never achieved this. The mission failed.

During a skirmish, Bill repeatedly faced intense enemy fire while rescuing his fallen comrades. For his actions, he was awarded the "Military Cross," England's second-highest award. Later, he would admit it was "A bridge too far."

Bill met Hilary Branfoot when he was invited to dinner at her father's house. His unit was training in Northumberland. Hilary's father was a shipbuilder in Sunderland during World War I. When they met, Hilary was with the Women's Land Army. The women in the Land Army took over farming jobs that men usually did while they fought abroad.

After a brief courtship and marriage, Bill and Hilary had Jeremy, Julius, Juliet, Jill, and Lucy in that order.

After the war, Bill spent most of his time in London advancing his career in journalism. His responsibilities at the Daily Telegraph became more demanding when he was promoted to editor, and he later ran for a seat in the House of Commons, which he won.

Hilary raised a small flock of Jacob sheep for show, wool, and meat. In the afternoons, she could be found in the south-facing sunroom, spinning wool and making hats and gloves while listening to tapes of bird songs. The girls learned to sew and knit at an early age.

Hilary had a special bond with her sheep. She named them, and when she called their names, they came to her. Though she loved her sheep, she was pragmatic. When it was time to take them to the butcher, she sent them off. The freezer always had a leg of lamb.

Born in a small maternity clinic in Aldington, Kent, Juliet attended a private girls' boarding school during her teenage years. She would take the train home on weekends to help her mom.

She rarely saw her father after he became a Cabinet Minister without portfolio in the Macmillan Administration.

His role was to serve as Press Secretary, managing the Prime Minister's media relations and editing the Daily Telegraph. He wrote speeches for figures like General Montgomery, Winston Churchill, and later for Margaret Thatcher and Lady Diana. Dennis Thatcher was his golf partner.

Juliet finished her education, moved to London, and enrolled at Miss Rose's Drama College.

From a young age, she had an appreciation for classic opera. After graduating from drama college, she explored opportunities with various opera companies. The Welsh Opera had an opening for an assistant stage manager and understudy. She applied and was accepted. Having the last name Deedes didn't hurt her at all.

It was a fantastic chance for her, and she embraced it eagerly, savoring every moment.

Her job was to work with the stage manager, choreographing the cast and performers. Everyone had to be on cue. If someone were sick or missing, she would take their place.

The opera became her family, where she felt she truly belonged. Sex, drugs, and alcohol filled the void that her real family failed to satisfy.

During her opera course, she had the opportunity to travel to South Africa and join an opera company there.

Her family was very familiar with South Africa. Her grandfather and great-uncle had both fought in the Boer War. Her father had been there multiple times on assignments from the newspaper. Her brother owned property and had a stake in a racehorse; it was also a great place to visit during the cold English winter months. She eagerly took the opportunity to keep that family tradition alive.

South Africa felt rejuvenated and new. She felt free from her aristocratic responsibilities.

Opera Ipe Tumbi was an African production featuring African singers and actors. She fell in love with the lead singer and had a romantic relationship. The problem was that it was during Apartheid, and it was illegal for a white woman to have sex with a black man. People started talking, and she feared she would face jail time and be discredited to her family. In the middle of the night, she ran, hoping to reach Durban to catch a ship home. During her escape, she met a missionary couple who gave her refuge. Spending time with them, they shared the Gospel, and she became a believer.

This missionary couple had ties to a mission hospital. Next to the hospital was an African Church with an African pastor. He was very charismatic and talented in speech, and she fell in love with him.

Unbeknownst to the pastor, Juliet believed she had received a vision from God to return home and pursue a Bible study course, followed by a nursing program. She planned to come back and marry the pastor, supporting him while working in the hospital. It all seemed so simple. She completed both the Bible study and nursing/midwife courses and graduated with honors.

There was a small mission church next to her family home in Aldington that she and her mother attended. She convinced the pastors there to invite the African pastor for a series of meetings and sermons.

The African pastor arrived with an associate from the church and stayed at Juliet's family home. There, Juliet shared her vision with him. He understood that with Apartheid, it could never happen. He didn't want the drama.

Juliet read books about famous women missionaries and wanted to become one. The son of the church's pastor attended medical school and became a doctor. His goal was to do medical missions. His first mission was to an orphanage in Nicaragua, and he invited Juliet to go with him. That was where we met.

I wrote as soon as I got home. She faithfully replied to each letter. I started pursuing this proper English woman in hopes of building a relationship. I thought that during spring break, when I had a week off, I would go to England to visit her. In my following letter, I asked if she would mind if I came.

She realized I had ambitions. She was right. The secret was out; she was glad I came over. I bought a plane ticket to England.

Juliet met me at Heathrow Airport in London. During our hour-and-a-half drive to her home in Aldington, we couldn't stop talking. I was captivated by the charming Kentish villages along the road. This was a completely different world for me. I met her immediate family and explored the local historic sites. It was a great time getting to know each other. We truly fell in love.

Returning to Eureka, I called her and invited her into my life. She came and stayed with close friends of mine. I asked her to marry me, and she accepted. Once she returned home to England, she began to question her decision. She was confused about God's calling to marry the pastor from Africa and asked me for more time. I was patient. Two weeks later, she called me back to say our marriage was back on.

We were married on April 7th, 1988.

We had hoped for a small English wedding, but her father wouldn't hear of it. He rented a large marquee to be placed in the garden, which was beautifully manicured with all the decorations. A caterer brought in plenty of delicious food to serve lords and ladies from all over England. Her extended family was there, including her sister's family from Australia. My mother and cousin Bonnie, along with Jon and Sharon, who came from California, were also present. Jon served as the best man.

We drove away from the property as crowds cheered, threw rice and confetti, while her brother blew the foghorn. We spent the first night in the Weymouth Ritz-Carlton honeymoon suite, and after a cup of tea, jumped into the Jacuzzi. The next day, we headed to Land's End, spending four nights at the renowned hotel and walking along the cliffs of western Cornwall.

My teaching career ended after three years. Budget cuts in Sacramento forced school districts to reduce costs. It didn't matter how strong your program was; the last program I was hired for was the first to be cut, and I eventually lost my job. I earned my teaching credential but never actually pursued a teaching career. I disliked the school's system structure, with too many rules and regulations, as well as backstabbing among staff. I didn't miss it at all because I was too independent and preferred working on my own.

Return To Vietnam

Our Floating House on Tri An Lake

Vietnam reopened for tourism. Seizing the opportunity, I gathered a group of Vietnam veterans to organize a trip. Once there, we asked if we could help with the rebuilding efforts. That led to the creation of an organization called "Vets With A Mission" (VWAM).

The government asked us to rebuild neglected orphanages all over Ho Chi Minh City. We put together teams of veterans eager to return home. It was a valuable form of therapy and helped many veterans achieve closure about their war experiences. So many wanted to go back that we organized two, sometimes three, trips a year.

My job was to arrive a week before the teams organized the projects and collect the necessary materials on site. The teams arrived and immediately began working. Time was set aside for individual members to visit the areas where they had fought. For most, this was a meaningful experience, providing closure from the war.

Our first project was the restoration of Polio Clinic #5, an orphanage for polio victims. Sister Jean Marie, a Catholic nun, managed it. She is the most energetic and selfless person I've ever known. She hated the communists and told me so many times. She wanted to leave Vietnam after the communists took control, but her dedication to the orphans kept her from leaving.

Our arrival was like a breath of fresh air for her. She was happy to see us and grateful for the help. Sometimes, it was awkward—we walked a thin line. I agreed that I didn't like communism either, but I had to watch what I said. The government allowed us to help but kept a close eye on us, following us everywhere. Listening ears could overhear every conversation.

The clinic was a old hotel with a broken-down swimming pool. The first thing Sister Jean Marie asked was to fix the pool for exercise therapy. Our team took care of it, and by the second visit, it was up and running.

There were vocational training programs so that when the orphans came of age, they could support themselves. The programs included a mechanic's shop, a sewing center, and a radio repair shop. We brought in tools for the mechanic and radio repair shops, as well as brand-new sewing machines for the sewing center.

Whenever we began or completed a project, the government would get involved by hosting a celebration. During these events, some government officials would stand up and praise the achievements of Communism.

At the end of our work at the polio orphanage, a dignitary was present. I learned he was a colonel, possibly in the VC or NVA, and had fought against us in many battles. Before I was introduced to him, he kept staring at me, sizing me up to the point that it became awkward.

When Sister Jean Marie introduced us, I told her to tell him that his troops were the bravest people I had ever met. Then he grabbed both of my hands and shook them vigorously, looking directly into my eyes. As he started his speech, the first thing he said was, "I just met the greatest friend I've ever had."

At the end of these celebrations, the men always held a chug-a-lug contest drinking Ba-Ba-Ba, the national beer. I drank him under the table.

To finish our work, we renovated the dormitories, kitchen, and laundry facilities. The communists believed we were becoming too familiar with Sister Jean Marie and told us to move on to other projects. We were at their mercy, and we reluctantly agreed.

I later learned that Sister Jean Marie retired from the polio clinic, moved back to the convent, and died in a motorcycle accident.

We restored five orphanages in the Saigon area over the following years. We met Dr. Hoa (pronounced "Wah"), head of the Pediatric Research Center. Dr. Hoa oversaw the Viet Cong medical corps during the war. After they won the war, she became disillusioned with communism and attempted to promote reforms aimed at changing the government.

Rural Maternity Clinic

She liked Juliet immediately and asked if we could help build maternity clinics in rural areas. Juliet and I accepted the challenge, moving to Vietnam to work in Dinh Quan Province. We lived in a floating house on Tri An Lake. I worked with teams of veterans building the clinic in the village of Phu Ngoc. Juliet collaborated with local medical staff, teaching them proper hygiene practices and assisting with deliveries.

And then there was Lan. She was in her late thirties. Lan was indispensable. She had worked at U.S. offices, either in the Embassy or MACV, during the war, where she became Americanized. She not only spoke English, but she also understood Americans. She didn't leave when the communists took over. She chose to stay with her family. Dr. Hoa hired her initially to cook for Juliet and me because she knew what we ate.

Lan became not only our language translator but also our cultural interpreter. She understood how Westerners thought and what they expected. She assumed the role of our social director in Saigon, organizing small after-hours events to keep us busy. She would prepare elaborate meals and deliver them to our boat so we could enjoy them on our open deck in privacy. She was slightly plump but lovely and a lot of fun to be around. She always acted like she appreciated us as much as we enjoyed her.

It was quite picturesque by the lake in Phu Ngoc. Dr. Hoa had a large mahogany wooden house built on top of a hill overlooking the lake, with the floating houses that had been rafted together visible below. She always arrived with a large entourage of servants and cooks. Many times, she'd have foreign dignitaries in tow and show us off to them.

I bought a Honda 125 motorcycle, and Juliet would ride on the back, sidesaddle, to and from the clinic in the village as I navigated the heavily pothole-riddled, muddy road. One time, when we were leaving the clinic and heading back to our houseboat, we drove past an open-air market. Juliet saw the beautiful, red and blue, handmade silk blouses hanging from a rod in one of the kiosks and asked me to stop so she could take a look. They were stunning, and I told her I'd buy her one, but she wanted to wait because she couldn't decide on a color.

One thing Juliet could never master while riding sidesaddle on the bike was knowing which way to lean during turns. I was in a hurry to get back because, after spending time at the market, we would be late for dinner. Dodging all the muddy, water-filled potholes, I made a left turn, and she leaned the opposite way, causing me to lose control and splash into a three-foot-deep pothole. I went headfirst into the mud.

Concerned about what had happened to her, I had to wipe mud out of my eyes to see her. When I finally looked, she was sitting on a small mound, scraping mud off her arm.

She looked at me as if nothing had happened and said, "You know, sweetheart, I think I'll get the blue one."

Dr. Hoa brought some of her people from Saigon to enjoy a day or two at the lake. A recently widowed mother of three visited her. The week before, her husband was walking down Saigon Street when a power line fell on him, instantly electrocuting him. We all felt sorry for her and tried to comfort her through this terrible ordeal.

Late in the afternoon, people from the house would come down and jump into the lake from one of the houses. They would get out, soap off, and jump back in to rinse for their daily bath. Inner tubes were available for those who couldn't swim. This poor lady came with them and entered the water, hanging onto an inner tube. She got out, soaped off, and then jumped into the inner tube, but because of the soap, she went right through and disappeared into the murky water.

Nobody paid attention until one of the other girls started screaming that the lady wasn't surfacing. When we finally realized, I looked at Hep, one of Dr. Hoa's male assistants, and we both jumped in to try to find her. The water was so murky that we couldn't see or locate her. After three attempts, I grabbed a rope and handed one end to Hep, and we stretched the rope along the bottom, trying to snag her. Hep ran right into her and brought her to the surface. We performed mouth-to-mouth to try to revive her. But it was too late. She was dead.

I wanted to give my youngest son, Christopher, the chance to experience the world. We arranged for him to stay with us in Vietnam for part of the summer and then return to finish his high school education. He liked the idea and invited a friend, Charlie. We bought him a ticket while visiting the States to raise money for our project. The flight from San Francisco to Bangkok, Thailand, was a grueling 18 hours. After a couple of days exploring the sights in Bangkok, we flew to Ho Chi Minh City, also known as Saigon. Chris and Charlie were mesmerized by the sights and sounds of such a foreign and exotic place. The animal market was their favorite; it had every animal you could find in Asia, including the cinnamon bear. They were less enthusiastic when I told them these animals were going to be eaten.

They thought our floating house on Tri An Lake was cool, but after ten days, Chris grew bored and wanted to go home. That wasn't our plan, but we didn't have the time to give them all our attention. Juliet kindly helped them pack their bags and flew back to Bangkok so they could catch a plane home to the States.

We had planned for Christopher the following year, but in the meantime, he fell in love and didn't want to come. It was probably for the best.

Dr. Lewis Zirkle of Orthopedics Overseas contacted me through Dr. Hoa, asking for help with their project to renovate the operating rooms at Saigon Orthopedic Hospital. Lew was a former Army surgeon who worked in active battle zones and began treating the wounded on the spot.

He asked if I could organize the shipment of three containers of medical equipment from Saigon Harbor to the hospital. By then, I was familiar with import and export procedures and offered my help.

What excited me about his request was the chance to help other organizations and generate income for an extended stay in the country.

With the help of one of Dr. Hoa's employees, we managed to move the containers to the hospital, but not before a standoff with customs officials who demanded a bribe. During the standstill, my helper told me that as it approached four o'clock, they would want to go home and release the containers. He was right, and the hospital received a new makeover.

Living on Tri An Lake in a floating village for two years, I learned how to build a sampan from Thu By, the local boat builder. The sampan, converted to sail, performed well. The boats were very popular with expats. I built five and gave them to my friends.

John Wade, an Australian working for British Petroleum, became a close friend. On weekends, he and his wife would visit and go sailing on the lake. One day, John asked me why, after everything I went through in the war, I wanted to come back.

Smiling, I said, "I haven't surrendered yet."

Juliet Awaiting My Return

Sailing Tri An Lake

PASSPORT PROBLEMS

Unknowingly, we wore out our welcome in Phu Ngoc. It started subtly at first. I went to see Thu By, my boat builder who had crafted five of my boats, and he wasn't the same—nervous and distant, as if he wanted me to leave. Something was wrong. Had the police visited him?

The clinic was finished, and Juliet was training local midwives on how to operate an autoclave for sterilizing medical instruments. She was performing a delivery when a problem occurred. She stepped out of the delivery room pale as a ghost, crying her eyes out, and said, "I blew it, I blew it."

I couldn't find out what happened from her. I only knew that the local midwives wanted nothing more to do with her.

Phuc, Dr. Hoa's nephew and part of her staff, refused to speak to me. It became very awkward when they asked us to go to Dinh Quan, the district capital, and find something to do there. We didn't know anyone there and lacked a support network, so we declined.

Having dinner with Dr. Hoa's staff by the lake, we were visited by the local police chief. Dr. Hoa was back in Saigon at the time. At first, he was polite and asked how we enjoyed the security they provided for us. I was confused by his question because, until then, I had never seen a policeman or any other official, except Dr. Hoa and her staff.

He demanded our passports. Sensing something was wrong, I hesitated to hand them over and told him so. His attitude suddenly shifted, insisting I had no choice. I was told to go to the police station the next day.

Juliet grew anxious about the encounter, wondering what I had involved her in. The staff was also upset. This had never happened before, and Dr. Hoa needed to be informed so she could resolve the issue. Her staff contacted her, and I was told she'd be out in a couple of days to handle the problem.

The next day, Lan and I went to the police station and sat in the waiting area. The police chief and another officer entered the room and took their seats behind the table.

They started the conversation by telling us they knew about the work at the health clinic. They watched us build the nicest building in the area and thought they deserved compensation for providing security. In other words, they were asking for a bribe because they believed we had plenty of money and wanted some of it.

Trying to be diplomatic, I asked them what kind of compensation they wanted. With a serious face and demeanor, they expected a brand-new Harley-Davidson police motorcycle.

Realizing their ignorance, I almost burst out laughing. Struggling to keep my composure, I explained that the clinic's total budget was $7,000. Buying a new Harley-Davidson police motorcycle would cost between $25,000 and $30,000, and honestly, we didn't have that kind of money.

Unfazed by my answer, Lan lost her temper and warned them they'd be in big trouble when Dr. Hoa returned. They calmly said they didn't care about Dr. Hoa and that there's no way to get our passports back without a brand-new Harley Davidson police motorcycle.

Lan said to me, "Let's go. Nothing more we can do here."

Juliet expected to see our passports in hand when we returned. After sharing the story of what had happened, she became distraught and wanted to leave. From then on, she was a nervous wreck, never imagining we'd be put in this position.

I was worried, but I thought it would work out once Dr. Hoa got involved. There was nothing to say or do to comfort Juliet. She wanted out. The conflict tore us apart. I loved Vietnam, believing it was where I wanted to spend the rest of my life. The last thing I wanted was to leave.

Dr. Hoa arrived a few days later and tried to negotiate with the police, but to no avail. Juliet was so depressed that she was near a nervous breakdown. I was disappointed but knew I had to get her out or take her home in a basket.

It took several weeks, but Dr. Hoa finally retrieved our passports after consulting with higher authorities. Our time in Vietnam was over. We boarded an Air France flight back to San Francisco.

Looking back, I realized that, unintentionally, we caused many problems in a rural area. Two white people in a sea of Vietnamese, throwing money around, sparked jealousy and conflict, with everyone wanting a piece of the pie. With the project finished and nothing more to give, it was better for us to leave so their lives could go back to normal. They didn't know how to say it politely. I was having too much fun to see it clearly.

Puerto Cabezas

Boat Shop, Nicaragua

Back in the States, we moved into a back bedroom with Jon and Sharon. I built a house for a friend. Juliet got a job as a nurse's aide at the local hospital while figuring out what to do next. The Vietnam experience had taken an unspoken toll on our relationship.

Dr. Robert Hamilton invited Juliet to join a medical expedition that would operate clinics in small villages along Nicaragua's Atlantic coast, near Pearl Lagoon. I accompanied them on the trip. Pearl Lagoon was a beautiful, peaceful place with a simple, subsistence lifestyle. I thought my boats from Vietnam might be helpful for the fishermen there.

After the Contra war, we arrived to find the Atlantic coast in ruins, with Miskito Indians returning to their villages from refugee camps in Honduras.

We spent ten days with the medical team on the lagoon, visiting four villages. Then we headed back to Managua, where Bob Trolese had a plan for Juliet and me. We ended up staying in Nicaragua for four years.

There was a small outreach on the Atlantic side in Puerto Cabezas. Bob asked me to develop an economic development project to help them recover. I wanted to go to Pearl Lagoon, but I accepted Bob's request and changed our plans. Puerto Cabezas is a town built on Bragman's Bluff by the Standard Fruit Company around the turn of the century. There was no safe harbor, just a large wharf extending into the Caribbean Sea.

Once, it was a thriving community with clean water, paved roads, schools, churches, and stores filled with desirable amenities. A railroad system connected the outlying areas. The houses were charming and comfortable, with fresh paint. By the time we arrived, it was in a state of disrepair, with termites having caused significant damage. The railroad was long gone, but one can still imagine what it once was.

During Somoza's era, the Atlantic region stayed autonomous. Authorities on the West Coast had no interaction with the Miskito Indians. The Miskito were proud and warlike, making it more trouble than it was worth to tame them and bring them into the fold.

When the Sandinistas overthrew Somoza, they believed it was their duty to include the Miskito Indians in the revolution. That's when problems began, and a counter-revolution ensued. It was a long and costly war that devastated most of the area and left coastal villages in ruins or abandoned.

With free elections, Violeta Chamorro defeated the Sandinistas. Peace began to return, and the Miskito returned to their villages from refugee camps in Honduras.

Juliet and I arrived in Puerto Cabezas shortly after the war. Juliet worked with the local outreach program, teaching English and spending time at the local hospital. The local outreach found us a house and helped us get settled. It was an old house built by the Standard Fruit Company, in much disrepair, but it was home.

I explored potential development opportunities and decided to support the local fishermen. I began building one of my Vietnamese sailing sampans in the lot next to our house. Boatbuilding was a big hit with the children in the neighborhood, and I was surrounded by kids trying to help.

Subsistence fishermen paddled out through the surf every morning in their ten-foot dugout canoes called cayucos. About a mile or two from the shore at their favorite fishing spots, they typically caught around twenty pounds of fish on a good day—just enough to sustain a modest life and support their families. One of my boats from Vietnam would give them an even greater range and capacity to catch fish.

After finishing the first boat, I took it to the beach where the local fishermen lived and worked. I watched them sail in their small cayucos with black plastic sails and got to know them, observing what they caught.

With the boat rigged, I received plenty of help launching it into the surf. I befriended Gilly, one of the fishermen, and asked if he wanted to go sailing. He jumped aboard, and we sailed out through the surf.

The boat was the envy of the fishermen, who asked how they could get one. This marked the beginning of the Nicaraguan fishing boat project.

Working with Gilly, we tested the boat and tweaked the sail design for the local waters. He asked if I could help his son, Gileto.

Gileto was a Contra fighter who had smuggled arms and ammunition to the Miskito Contras during the war. He used boats to smuggle and knew the local waters like the back of his hand. We spent time sailing and fishing, testing out this new boat. We sailed down the coast thirty-five miles to Princa Polka. The fishing was good, and the people wanted to see our boats.

Gileto kept fishing in those waters for a couple of weeks. When he returned, he said he had made good money but felt we needed a bigger boat with a higher freeboard for rough weather. I agreed and began building our second boat, making it three feet longer and adding an extra strake. When it was finished, we launched the new boat at Lamlaya, a village at the end of an estuary that feeds into the Wawa and Karata Lagoons.

It was a fifteen-mile sail across the calm waters of Karata Lagoon from Lamlaya to the open ocean through Wawa Bar. We wanted to scout ahead before crossing the bar and facing a nine-mile beat to Puerto Cabezas in rough seas.

At the mouth of the Wawa River, the breaking waves on the outer bar didn't seem too bad. Moving along with eighteen-knot winds and a receding tide, we would soon be past the point of no return. We were heading due east on a hard beat, approaching the breaking waves. Cutting through the white water slowed us down, but with plenty of rocker in our hull, we managed fine.

It was during the break that I realized our new twenty-one-foot, open, gaff-rigged sailboat was about to face its first challenge. Six- to eight-foot waves were breaking on the outside, and we had to sail through them. Turning around in this chaotic sea would be disastrous. Nicaraguan bull sharks beneath the surface could make it deadly.

Reaching the break, we faced eight-foot waves. You've seen photos of windsurfers soaring as they ride breaking waves; that's what happened with a twenty-one-foot wooden sailboat. Sailing at six knots, we surged up over the crest of the first eight-foot wave. Completely airborne, we came down so hard I thought the mast would punch through the bottom of the boat.

We recovered just in time to face the next wave. Airborne again, we took another hard crash, but everything held together. We beat the third wave of the set before she broke. Suddenly, we were outside the break. We survived.

Sailing due east for a mile, we tacked north toward Puerto Cabezas. It was getting late in the afternoon. The wind increased to twenty knots. The seas were rougher than hell.

Overpowered by strong winds, I dropped the headsail. The strong current from north to south meant we weren't making any progress. What we gained from sailing was washed away by the current.

Adding to our dilemma, I was getting seasick and realized we'd be out here all night—the only boat I could see. If something were to happen, there would be no one to help.

I started to think this might not be such a good idea. The only choice was to go back inside and wait for a better day. That choice also came with risks. Surfing eight-foot waves is more dangerous than sailing through them, especially with those bull sharks lurking beneath the surface. It was decision time.

While bailing out water, I glanced back at Gileto. He didn't look too well either. I pointed back toward the shore through the bar, and he nodded in response.

There was no way I was going to sail back through those waves with the full main up. We'd be sailing on a broad reach with twenty knots of wind, moving like a bat out of hell. We were sure to broach on the first wave. I dropped the main and raised the headsail. Gilly turned the helm back through the waves and sharks as nightfall was approaching. Our chances were slim.

Approaching the break, I held on tight. It was do or die. Looking behind, I saw a big one was on us. We gained speed and rode this monster. If the nose was buried in the trough, it was all over. This was quite a ride. It was all Gileto could do to handle the helm, keeping us on a straight course.

We surfed past the break into calmer waters. Although it was exhilarating, our problems were far from over as we entered the Wawa River.

The wind was howling, and the headsail was pulling us along. I was satisfied with the setup, but Gileto wanted to raise the main to make better time. Against my better judgment, I hauled up the main and peak halyards. No sooner had the main gone up than we took a hit, knocking us down. The boat swamped and filled with water. I had to lower the sails before we flipped over, with no way to right the boat. What a mess we were in now!

Lowering my weight to bring the sails down, I released the halyards and thank God the sails came down safely.

Now it was time to bail. It took twenty minutes to bail out while the current pushed us back into the break. With the boat half empty, I raised the headsail to keep us heading toward land. The sun set as we passed through Wawa Village and entered the river. It was going to be a night with heavy overcast.

Back in the river, protected from the wind, I raised the main sail and headed toward the lights of Karata Village. We rounded the point into Wawa Lagoon, and it was all dead reckoning from there. The wind eased into a gentle breeze as we searched for the creek's entrance, which would lead us back to Lamlaya.

Barely making progress, we entered the creek, and the wind completely died down. Manning handmade oars, I rowed the last three miles while Gileto steered us home.

We arrived in Lamlaya at two in the morning, secured the boat, and walked two miles back to Puerto Cabezas to my run-down home. If the wild dogs didn't get us, I would soon climb under my mosquito netting to get some well-earned sleep.

Kevin Sanderson to the Rescue

Through Bob Trolese, I met Kevin Sanderson during a trip to Managua. Kevin was the Latin American Director for World Relief, a faith-based disaster relief and development agency based in Baltimore, Maryland. At our first meeting, I told him I was starting a fisheries boat-building project for returning refugees from Honduras. He liked the idea and came over to take a look.

Bob Trolese passed away this year from cancer. It was a significant loss, and he will be deeply missed. He was a close friend and a tireless advocate for the poor in Latin America.

I took Kevin out sailing to the local fishing grounds. After catching a good number of fish, he decided to finance two boats. This marked the start of a long and prosperous relationship that continues to this day.

I secured funding to rent a workshop with electricity near the airport. I hired three local Creole boys and set up a shop to teach them how to build boats so they could continue the trade after I left. Kokie Lampson was my leading man and right-hand, a very dependable person. I couldn't have done what we did without him. Trouble started right away when I had to fire another boy who stole tools and resold them.

After finishing two boats, we took them to the beach where local fishermen lived and started the fishing association. We picked captains, and they chose their crews, usually family members.

A German group visited our boat shop and ordered a thirty-two-foot version of one of our fishing boats. We extended the lines, and once finished, the boat handled superbly. The Germans sailed it home, extremely satisfied.

Wayne, an Australian man, wanted a thirty-two-foot boat so he could trap lobsters in the Miskito Cays. He named her the Creole Princess. I sailed with Wayne many times to the Cays. She was a great boat and a pleasure to sail. Wayne spent two years in Nicaragua. When he left, he sold the Creole Princess to a Japanese buyer.

Wayne and I have maintained our friendship over the years, visiting each other in Amsterdam, Hungary, and Spain. We both became struggling writers.

I was approached by a Japanese man named Akia Seko. Akia worked with a Japanese group developing fisheries. Impressed with our boats, he contracted with our team to build a fleet of nine 21-foot sailboats and two 32-footers. They added a 5-hp outboard Yamaha to the 21-footers and 25-hp engines to the 32-footers.

Launching the boats from the beach through the surf was wearing down the boats. Akia told me there was funding available through the Japanese Embassy to build a harbor. A delegation of Japanese officials visited Puerto Cabezas to inspect the project.

The Harbor Project Disaster

The idea was to expand Land Creek just north of town, where they would build a jetty and a docking facility a mile up the creek. It sounded good until they told me they worked with the local government. I got nervous because I knew the local government was corrupt, and I told them so.

They dismissed my concern and said they would donate $300,000 to the project in $100,000 installments. They planned to monitor the first installment with the local government, and if everything were satisfactory, they would proceed with the project. Still feeling uneasy, I shrugged my shoulders and told them it was their money. They asked if I would manage the project. I considered it, and after some hesitation, I reluctantly agreed.

The Japanese set up an accounting system, and a young engineer from the mayor's office was assigned to work with me. Our first task was to buy large rocks from the interior to line our new jetty. There was a village thirty miles inland, surrounded by large volcanic rocks. Akia, the young engineer, and I drove out to the village and asked how much they wanted for their rocks. They told us $100 each. We were thinking about $5 each. We tried to negotiate, but the village chief wasn't budging. We conferred among ourselves, and the engineer told us not to worry—give them a week, and they'll lower the price.

In the meantime, we built a pile driver to drive logs along each side of the channel and started working. One of the boys climbed to the top of the pile driver, fell off, broke his neck, and died. It was a tragic event. At the funeral, it was customary to give the family a monetary gift. I gave a hundred dollars.

The village chief visited us and said he would sell us rocks for $5 each. We signed a contract and hired local trucks to start hauling rocks. The loaded trucks heading to the beach stopped at a bridge crossing. Two men with AK-47s demanded a 30% toll for crossing. The Japanese decided to go ahead with the payment. I wondered how far this project would go.

The beach people strongly insisted that we only hire them to build the harbor and jetty. They didn't want outsiders working on the project. I hired a local guy who seemed hardworking to supervise the laying of rocks. Come Mother's Day, he demanded double pay. He was told we didn't pay double on Mother's Day. He quit. After a week of hard work, the beach people no longer wanted to work, so we hired workers from nearby villages.

A quarter of the project is complete, and we have used the first $100,000 allotment. It was discovered that the mayor had "borrowed" $25,000 of the funds to open two new restaurants in the area. That was it for the project. The Japanese backed out.

The fishing association didn't always succeed. To participate, each captain gave twenty percent of his catch to the group. That twenty percent was used to replace fishing gear and maintain the boats.

Those captains didn't want to give up the money. Sometimes they'd go somewhere else to sell their fish, come back empty-handed, and claim they hadn't caught anything.

The captains were responsible for applying bottom paint to protect their vessels from wood-boring worms. When it was time for one of the captains to paint his boat's bottom, he refused. I told him I would take his boat and give it to someone else. He attacked me, swinging his machete. I stood my ground, daring him to cut me. He backed down.

Junior's Betrayal

Junior was my top worker in the boat shop. He learned the boat-building techniques quickly, so I didn't have to watch him constantly. One day, while I was out, a man came into the shop looking for a 32-footer. Junior told the man he could build it much cheaper outside the shop. The man and Junior agreed. The man paid Junior and bought the lumber so he could make the boat in the man's yard.

I was completely unaware of the contractual agreement until Junior showed up at the shop, telling me he had messed everything up and needed help. I suggested they bring what they'd completed so far into the shop, and we would finish the boat there. But it was too late—the man was furious, spreading the word all over town that the project was a scandal and Junior had ripped him off.

To make matters worse, Junior had spent half the money on other things and had nothing left to finish the project. At that time, I didn't have the money either, so I had to let it go. I felt bad because Junior was likely to go to jail.

The Ambulance Boat

Kevin called me from Managua and said he wanted a 32-foot boat with an engine. He had money to use as an ambulance to serve the outer villages. We built the same hull design as the sailboats and, with a friend's help, installed a 28-hp Wester Beke diesel. It turned out very nice. The problem was that it wasn't fast enough, so they ended up using a Panga with an outboard. That gave us a motor launch to cruise around in. Juliet and I used it to explore the lagoons on weekends. There will be more to this story later.

Over the course of four years working in Puerto Cabezas, we built eighteen 21-foot boats and five 32-footers. It was idyllic to watch the fleet sail out to the fishing grounds. Women fish buyers gave the captain of each boat a pound of shrimp for bait, ensuring they had first choice of the catch upon their return. Along with the fish buyers and me, a crowd gathered at four in the afternoon, waiting for the fleet to come back. On the horizon, we saw a stick emerge, soon turning into a sail. The buyers argued over which boat belonged to them. Before the boats cleared the surf, the buyers rushed into the water and jumped onto their boats, shouting with joy as they saw their catch. I never tired of witnessing this event.

Academics from around the world came to study our fleet. The head of U.S. Fisheries visited us, and I took him sailing. A team of fishing adventurers visited to see if they could include us in their tours.

A group of investors from Texas read a false report that tons of fish were swimming off the Nicaraguan coast, waiting to be harvested. They came to investigate and visited me at the boat shop while I was repairing one of the boats. Impressed with what they saw, they asked me to show them my operation. It was close to four o'clock, so I took them down to the beach to watch the fleet return. Delighted by what they witnessed, they invited me out to dinner to discuss possible investments.

I met them at Cresfa's restaurant and sat down as they ordered drinks. They asked me how I had set up the operation while we were ordering dinner. Later, we sat sipping another drink when one man looked at me and said he had a hundred thousand dollars he wanted to invest in fisheries. He asked about the best place to put it and how secure it would be to get a good return. His eyes lit up when I told him I could guarantee his investment the next day. Excitedly, he asked, "How's that?"

I told him, "Be at the airport at seven o'clock in the morning and catch the first flight out of here, taking your money with you."

They followed my advice but never paid my consulting fee.

After four years, Juliet no longer wanted to live in third-world countries. She was burned out and aimed to rebuild her life in Western culture.

After we left, you wouldn't have known we had ever been there. Everything fell apart over time. The harbor was never constructed. But it wasn't all bad news. I had a great time, with plenty of sailing adventures and all the fresh shrimp and fish I could eat

Adios England, Hello Virginia

England, Greece, and the Seychelles

After our time in Nicaragua, we moved back to England and settled in Oxford, where we rented a small apartment. Juliet needed to renew her nursing credentials.

An international development organization invited me to enroll in a master's program at Oxford Brookes University, with the potential for employment afterward. I didn't realize it at the time, but they hoped that Juliet's father, due to his reputation, would become a supporter of their organization and offer assistance.

Midway through the course, the organization was caught making inappropriate expenditures. They collapsed, and I lost my job. I stayed on to complete the course at Oxford Brookes.

The Development Practices course is designed for field workers who lack formal academic qualifications but wish to earn a master's degree, with practical field experience accounting for half of the credits. When applying for grants, having an MDP on your resume was advantageous. Part of the curriculum required students to travel to a developing country and conduct research on mitigation. I was selected to lead a group of five classmates to Nicaragua.

Landing in Managua, I reached out to Kokie in Puerto Cabezas to reserve our motor launch for taking these students to outlying villages for research. He said, No problem. Four days later, when I arrived there, I was glad to see him and asked about the boat. He explained that there was a problem—the man hired to watch the boat in Lamlaya had stolen it, and no one knew its whereabouts.

That messed everything up. We did our best to get by, and I asked Kokie to do whatever he needed to find the boat, making sure that when he caught the thief, he would go to jail.

When we left Nicaragua, there was still no word on the whereabouts of the boat or the thief.

Greece and the Boat Refit

After finishing the course, I reached out to Robert, whom I had helped on the schooner in Vietnam. He was refitting an older 110-foot ship that the owners wanted to use as a dive platform in the Indian Ocean. I asked if he needed any assistance, and Robert invited me to come by. I enjoyed Greece and working on the ship.

Juliet visited twice a month to work in the galley. We took the time to explore the countryside, visiting the area's historic sites. I saw an opportunity for my oldest son, Jamie, to come and help with the refit. He could earn some money and see a bit of Greece.

Jamie was a true cowboy. I don't know how he ended up that way since I was a surfer and never imagined, even in my wildest dreams, that one of my kids would become a cowboy. When I picked him up at Athens airport, he didn't dress down for the European crowd. Out of the gate came this big ol' cowboy with a big hat, boots, Levi's jeans, a Western shirt, and a brass buckle leather belt.

This American cowboy made advances on the cute British girl they hired to run the galley. She couldn't resist, and soon they were sharing a cabin. It was nice to see them take a few days off and travel through Greece. I would've gone along, but didn't want to get in the way.

In the end, their blooming relationship didn't last. Jamie returned to the States to start a horse ranch with his mother and focus on his art. The charming British girl went back to England to drive a truck.

Robert's eccentricity caused an argument with the owners, which led to their firing him. They hired a new Dutch captain to oversee the refit. He was somewhat eccentric, but nothing like Robert. After finishing the refit, they needed a delivery crew and asked if I would help take her to the Seychelles. It was one of the best moments of my life.

The Voyage to the Seychelles

We raised anchor late one afternoon in Piraeus, Greece, and set out for Port Said, Egypt. The new captain was extremely seasick throughout the trip. It took five days for the paperwork to clear customs and for a canal captain to arrange passage through the canal.

Traveling through the Suez Canal and the Red Sea felt mystical, a stark contrast from one side to the other. The west side was lush and green, while the east was a barren desert with not a blade of grass in sight. At the end of the Red Sea, we arrived in Djibouti. The pilot's book called it the "grimmest place on earth," and it truly was.

Since we were delayed there for a week, we decided to explore the town. Along with the French Foreign Legion, there were 12-foot by 12-foot screens on every corner, blasting MTV music nonstop. In the downtown area, bar after bar was full of prostitutes. Because I was married, I kept myself busy by drinking and dancing with the girls.

We fueled up, refreshed the galley, and headed east from the Gulf of Aden. There, I caught the biggest fish of my life: an eighty-pound Mahi-Mahi. It made for great eating.

We rounded the horn of Africa through the Socotra Straits and headed south toward the Seychelles, immediately feeling the swell start to grow. It wasn't long before we faced howling winds and 40- to 50-foot seas, which lasted a total of eight days. Most of us were seasick throughout the storm, but we still had to fulfill our duties. It was tough.

Two days before we reached the Seychelles, the seas subsided to a flat calm, making the rest of the ride enjoyable. The sight of land never felt so good.

Arriving on the main island of Mahé, we docked in Victoria, the capital, and handed the ship over to the owners.

I stayed for two more days but was ready to go home, back to Juliet. I received my payment and boarded a Kenya Airways flight to London, with stops in Nairobi and Amsterdam.

Two years later, pirates seized the ship near the Comoros Islands. The crew was ransomed, but the Indian Ocean Explorer was never heard from again.

Marital Problems

Back in Oxford, my marriage was struggling. Things got so uncomfortable that I ended up sleeping on the floor in the living room.

"Oh hell, did I blow another one?"

I had planned to return to Nicaragua to finish my master's dissertation on fish folk when she told me she needed some time alone. The next day, I flew to Central America, arriving just after Hurricane Mitch had devastated the Atlantic coast and northern Nicaragua.

I asked Kevin Sanderson, director of World Relief, if he needed any help. He assigned me to work on several housing projects along the Honduran-Nicaraguan border.

My first job was to show big donors what World Relief was doing with their money. Kevin gave me a Toyota Land Cruiser and directions on where to go. It was rough country up there—most of the roads had been washed out.

After three days bouncing around in the Land Cruiser with one of the donors, he said he'd seen enough. He'd trust my word on the other projects and wanted to go home.

While working for Kevin, I attempted to focus on my dissertation, but I struggled to get into it. I felt bummed about leaving Juliet in England, not knowing what was going to happen. Eventually, I learned from Kokie that he'd found the motor launch safe in Lamlaya, even though it was severely damaged. The thief was rotting in jail.

Several people I knew wanted boats to sail on lakes and along the coast. To pass the time, I built three of them and stayed drunk most of the time. During this period, I met Dale Dagger, a surfer from Southern California. He had built a catamaran and sailed down the coast, stopping at popular surf spots. He had arrived in San Juan del Sur, running surf tours with his boat. Dale invited me to stay at his workshop, where I built a boat for a Dutchman.

San Juan del Sur was a popular spot for college students wanting to learn Spanish. Someone in town had established a Spanish program where students stayed with local families while immersing themselves in the language and community. They not only studied, but the town was lively with dance halls and open-air bars facing the bay. It was the place to be, and Dale fit right in with his surf tours.

Young college kids stopped by to visit the boat shop and were amazed that this gringo was there building boats. Word spread, and I had a steady stream of visitors. Nearly every night, I was invited out to socialize so they could hang out with a "legend." Staggering back drunk to my room, I realized I couldn't keep this up forever.

I told Dale about the motor launch we had in Puerto Cabezas. If he wanted it, I'd ask Kevin to donate it as part of an economic development project. Dale liked the idea, so I called Kevin, who approved it. Dale and I flew to Puerto Cabezas and met with Kokie to get the boat ready for the trip. Dale motored down the east coast of Nicaragua, up the San Juan River, across Lake Nicaragua to Rivas, then hired a truck to haul it to San Juan del Sur. There, he did a complete refit and resumed his surf tours.

The constant pain from my failed marriage never disappeared. I decided I had to face Juliet and flew back to England, hoping to resolve things.

When I arrived, she had gotten a job at William and Harvey Hospital in the maternity clinic. She had bought a bicycle and pedaled the two miles to work and back in the miserable English weather.

Showing up at her doorstep in Cowley, England, I was met with a cold reception. Conversation was sparse as she kept busy scurrying around the apartment. Still sleeping on the floor, I decided to give an ultimatum. In the morning, she entered the room as I was tying my shoes.

Looking up, I said, "Sweetheart, I've been here before, and I don't want to bother you anymore if you don't want to be together. I'll leave you alone today, make arrangements, take you out to dinner tonight, and then head out tomorrow."

I returned late in the afternoon, took a shower, and got ready for dinner. We walked under the Ring Road Bridge to the other side of the Range Rover plant, where there was a nice restaurant.

During dinner, with little conversation, she looked up and said, "I don't want to break up."

I answered, "What do you want to do?"

She wanted to move to the U.S. I agreed, and we decided to look in San Diego, where my family lived. I knew I could make it work there.

Life in Virginia

In San Diego, our living costs were too high for us. We needed to find another place.

I met Hal Moore in Nicaragua. He was a photojournalist working for Reuters News Service, covering the Banana Wars. He had come to Puerto Cabezas and written an article about my fishing fleet. Now he had returned to the States because of his health. I kept in touch with him through letters and phone calls.

He had moved to Alexandria, Virginia, to be with his wife, a speechwriter for the Secretary of the Interior. In our conversations, I mentioned that I was having a hard time finding a place to settle in the States. He suggested that we stay with him and explore his area.

Juliet liked the idea because her parents were aging, and she felt the East Coast was closer to England than the West Coast. Hal took us to

Maryland's Eastern Shore, and we enjoyed the area.

He told me about a business deal he was about to start with people in Texas, involving the development of specialty charcoal for barbecues. He had run into Danny Gill in Urbanna, Virginia. Danny was considering the same idea, and during their conversation, they decided they should meet.

Urbanna is a small town with a population of 500, situated on the southern bank of the Rappahannock River, about three hours south of Washington, D.C. Hal hadn't been there before, but he asked if we wanted to check it out. We agreed, and Hal called Danny to arrange a lunch meeting for the next day.

Danny's farm was on LaGrange Creek, a tributary of the Rappahannock. He owned eighty acres, raised eighty head of cattle, and had thirty hogs. It was a beautiful area, still kept in a simpler time.

Danny was an excellent host, with an impressive spread laid out for lunch. A historian of the area, he shared how Urbanna was first established in 1680 as a revenue port to ship tobacco to Europe. His stories were intriguing, keeping us on the edge of our seats.

He was working on a "retort" (a vessel or chamber that turns wood into charcoal) to produce specialty charcoal for barbecues and asked if I wanted to help. We could live on the farm for free until we decided what to do next. Juliet felt optimistic about the possibility of coming here to start a new life.

Juliet returned to England due to a green card issue and needed to reapply. While she was away, I traveled to Eureka to pick up some of our belongings, then flew to Richmond, where Danny was buying used commercial kitchen equipment to refurbish and sell. After a day of loading a lot of kitchen gear into his trailer, we headed to his farm, and I moved into the back room of his house.

Danny was unlike anyone I'd ever met before, very laid back. Time didn't matter to him. He followed a loose schedule, which wasn't my style.

Every day at four o'clock, he drove into town to visit the local pubs and didn't come home until closing time. I was expected to come along. The advantage of going into town with Danny was that he was a local icon and everyone knew him. Due to our association, it didn't take long to become acquainted with the local characters.

We spent time developing the retort he had designed. My task was to take his design to the local metal fabricator for manufacturing the parts. After they were made, we assembled and fired it up. It worked perfectly. Then he lost interest, and I was left with nothing to do. So, I built one of my boats to sail on the river.

Impressed with my boat, Danny left me alone to go sailing until Juliet returned. I had to complete a significant amount of paperwork to process Juliet's reissued green card. Once the paperwork was finished, Juliet came to our new home, a travel trailer Danny had on the property.

After Juliet arrived, I bought an old Honda Civic from one of Danny's neighbors for $500 to get around. That's how we started fresh in a new area with new people.

Danny eventually opened a restaurant downtown Urbanna for his daughter. The restaurant was quite successful, a thriving business. One evening, he went to take a nap in his office and never woke up.

Our finances were running low, and we needed an income for our new start. Thanks to Uncle Wyndham, Juliet was able to rent out the house she owned at 95 North Road in Hythe, England.

Once she arrived in Urbanna, things weren't working out at Danny's farm. We needed to find a place of our own. In the meantime, Juliet found a job as a nurse's aide at the convalescent hospital in Saluda, the county seat. I found carpentry work to keep body and soul together.

A letter arrived from the renters of Juliet's house in England. They wanted to buy it. We sold the house and purchased a lot in Urbanna to build on. Land was cheap, and we had plenty of money left over to build our home, plus some.

It was a wonderful neighborhood with friendly neighbors. We felt positive about this move and our new life.

Juliet worked at the nursing home until she passed her exam to become an RN. She met another nurse from the Virginia Department of Health who was working part-time at the nursing home. She told Juliet about a part-time nursing opening at the Virginia Health Department. Juliet applied and was accepted.

We purchased another lot with the money left over from the sale in England. I went to the bank to request a loan to build a house on it. After completing the paperwork, they approved my request and loaned me the money. I was now in the speculative home-building business.

After some time, Juliet was offered the head nursing position at the Health Department office in Mathews County, thirty miles away. She accepted the job and became a full-time employee.

She loved her new job and worked very diligently at it. I sold the first house, bought another lot, and built a new house. I then sold that one and purchased two more lots.

Then we were hit by Hurricane Isabel. We had never experienced a hurricane before and had no idea what to expect. It hit us with full force.

It was terrifying. Large trees kept falling everywhere, blocking our roads. Luckily, no trees hit our houses. It took two days, with neighbors working together with chainsaws, to clear a path to the main road.

Devastation was widespread. The residents along the river were hit hardest, losing most of their docks and boats. It took a long time to recover from that storm.

Shortly after the hurricane, we found out that Juliet's mother's cancer had come back, and she was back in the hospital. Juliet rushed to be with her for the rest of her days. Three years later, she hurried back again to say goodbye to her sick 94-year-old father, who left a legacy through his achievements. His death was front-page news in all the English newspapers.

Wanderlust

The *Mermaid*

Sailing on the Seas of Time

Living my new life in Virginia, I read a story in a sailing magazine about a fishing and sailing fleet on the island of Carriacou in the Grenadines. Having owned a fleet of fishing sailboats in Nicaragua, I was intrigued by the workboats under sail on Carriacou. I wondered how others made a living that way. I knew the struggle firsthand, having watched my fleet fall apart after four years of trying to keep it alive.

I bought a ticket to Grenada to explore it. Checked into Mitchell's Guest House in St. George, Grenada—before turning in, I went back to the dock to find *Adelaide B*, the cargo schooner I was supposed to take to Carriacou.

I found Captain Bully of the *Adelaide B,* a large 24-year-old West Indian, and told him I needed a ride to Carriacou. I explained that I was writing a story about workboats, including his own. I noticed the sails weren't hanked on and asked if we would be sailing. He said the sails had ripped in the last storm, so he was motoring. When I asked how long ago that happened, he told me his father had retired two years ago, and he had taken over the boat.

He never explicitly said it, but the feeling was that no sails had been raised since he took charge. Disappointed but determined to keep going, I told him I would return by 8:30 a.m. so we could leave at nine.

At 8:30 a.m., as I left St. George Harbor, many sailboats motored in for a large regatta. While I enjoyed watching the regatta, I was also pleased to observe the dynamics of the workboat fleet. Who knew the importance of local regattas in keeping working fleets alive and motivated?

The trip from Grenada to Carriacou was exhausting. With wind gusting over thirty-five knots directly against us as we fought the waves, the decks were flooded—so much for my nostalgic cruise on a sailing cargo hauler.

In the lee of Carriacou, the ocean calmed down. Tying up at the Carriacou dock was no easy task—the wind was blowing so strongly that the crew struggled with the lines. The fact that they'd consumed three bottles of rum during the trip didn't help.

Another observation: the constant use of cell phones. I thought we were witnessing the death throes of tradition.

Leaving *Adelaide B*, I asked for directions to John's Unique Resort. I found the place without much trouble. Checking in, I noticed a couple sitting on the patio.

I inquired if they knew John Smith, the captain of the *Mermaid*, who is reportedly one of the oldest workboats on the island.

"Yeah, everyone knows John Smith. He's a wild guy. He's around somewhere."

A passerby overheard me and said Smith had been seen sailing his small dory in Tyrell Bay that morning. I hired a taxi for $10 U.S. and headed to Tyrell Bay.

At the French restaurant, I was told to check with Billy Bones, an American who owned Windward Marine. He lived up the hill next to the butcher's shop. Cautiously approaching what I believed was Billy Bones' house.

I knocked on the door. Billy Bones opened it, wearing shorts held up by a safety pin. He had a glass eye, four days' worth of beard growth, and a ruddy complexion from spending years at sea in the sun.

"I'm Bob Means. I'm searching for John Smith. I'm writing a story about the workboats of Carriacou."

Bones took me out onto his overhanging porch overlooking Tyrell Bay and pointed out John's boat, the *Mermaid*. His dinghy was beside it, and Bones said he would come up soon since he had invited him earlier in the day.

Looking out over the bay, I saw twenty or thirty cruising yachts, a mix of catamarans and monohulls. I thought, "For the cruising crowd, this must be paradise."

I noticed a small double-ended dinghy sailing with a cat sprit rig heading toward the dock at Carriacou Marina. Bones said John Smith's boats didn't have engines. The *Mermaid* had been without an engine since her launch thirty-two years ago.

John bought the *Mermaid* twenty-five years ago from Zephrine McLawrence, who had built it for Lynton Rigg. When Lynton Rigg died in 1964, he willed the boat back to Zephrine.

Lynton Rigg single-handedly revitalized boatbuilding on Carriacou. He retired from Burgess & Rigg Marine Architects and Builders of Massachusetts in the late 1950s and relocated to the southern Caribbean.

When Rigg arrived in Carriacou, the island's economy was stagnant.

Modern cruisers saw it as a paradise, but for the locals who lived and worked there, life had always been a struggle. Since Columbus, the goal has never been to find paradise but to seek economic gain. Disease, shipwrecks, starvation, and ongoing military conflict had been the norm for hundreds of years.

The first to settle in the Grenadines after disease nearly wiped out the native population were the Huguenots. In the late 1700s, the British Crown sent Scottish shipbuilders to construct sailing ships for inter-island trade and fishing. The local woods were ideal for this industry.

The names indicate this migration. The current shipbuilders are McLawrence, Stewart, McFarlane, Compton, and McDonald. Their reputation lasted until the early 1900s, when a tough economy and the rise of steam power affected their prominence.

To revive the maritime tradition on Carriacou, Rigg designed and built the *Mermaid*, a 56-foot gaff-rigged cutter, which is considered a workboat. Rigg organized a workboat regatta with a $500 prize for first place. He believed that competition would boost the local economy more than anything else, and he was right. The *Mermaid* won the first regatta and the next nine years in a row. Soon after, signs of other boats emerging to compete with this newcomer began to appear. To support themselves in this renewed spirit, they utilized their boats for fishing, transporting passengers, and hauling cargo.

John Smith climbed the trail leading to Bones' cliffside home. I introduced myself and explained my intentions. Our conversation ranged from similar maritime adventures to mutual acquaintances and experiences during the Vietnam War.

Local history emerged, emphasizing the importance of the *Mermaid* and her role in revitalizing traditions and rebuilding the fishing industry with the aid of sail. The *Mermaid* was so cherished that she appeared on Grenada's 35-cent stamp.

John and I agreed on a three-day cruise to the outer islands.

Before my cruise, I wanted to visit the windward side of the island and explore the boatbuilding and fishing communities. I met Benson while he was working on his boat on the beach. Hundreds of boats, ranging from

6 feet to 110 feet, had been built on this beach among the tangle of trees and mangroves.

Benson won the Bequia Regatta last year in the Stern Boat Division. Stern boats were initially designed for whaling, a practice that continues to occur in the area.

The next morning, I met John Smith at the market in Tyrell Bay. We bought supplies for a three-day trip. Rowing out to the *Mermaid*, I encountered Winger, John's small black dog, who acted as if he'd been abandoned for weeks. I was shown my bunk and stored my gear while John put away the provisions.

The *Mermaid* was my dreamboat. She was a seasoned veteran of workboats with 35 years of experience. Her deck showed paint of various colors, and the deckhouse bore signs of heavy use and modifications. With pre-sail chores complete, it was time to hoist the anchor and set sail.

It's challenging to get used to someone else's boat, especially one with as much personality as the *Mermaid*. Adjusting to halyards, topping lifts, and sheets can be difficult. John's patience with a new crew member, as he explained things he usually handled single-handedly, could be pushed to its limit.

This cruise was no different. With the wind gusting up to thirty knots, it was a relief to finally have the sails up and sit back under the aft awning, watching the *Mermaid* sail ride the waves unattended.

Our destination was Chatham Bay on the sheltered side of Union Island. Winger pressed close against my hip to earn a few affectionate strokes. John started the conversation by sharing his thirty-five years at sea, twenty-five of them aboard the *Mermaid*.

John's life began on Long Island Sound, where he sailed as a young man. He never recovered from his experience in the U.S. Navy as a corpsman during the Vietnam War. His work aboard a hospital ship, caring for young Marines—many of whom never survived—became more than he could handle.

After receiving an honorable discharge, he tried to regroup in his hometown. But memories kept haunting him, so he headed south. He crewed on many boats and eventually ended up in the Southern Caribbean with the *Mermaid.*

The *Mermaid* became his full-time job. He started by chartering and took onshore work whenever opportunities arose. An old wooden boat without an engine required numerous repairs, including new sails, rigging, paint, and hull fixes. One task he undertook to meet these needs was managing a nudist colony. That's where he met Raquel Welch.

We discussed loves won and lost, including one he never got over—a beautiful Norwegian woman he eventually followed to Norway. The cold was too much for him, so he returned to the warmth and comfort of the tropical sea and his beloved *Mermaid.*

John had survived two bottles of rum being shattered over his head and fought off a knife attack from an anguished lover. He'd been kicked out of numerous bars, pubs, and marine establishments, some of which he still isn't allowed back into.

A weathered old sea captain at fifty-five, he was one of the best boat handlers I had the privilege of sailing with. Our three-day cruise took us to Union Island and Saline Bay on the island of Mayreau.

The *Mermaid* went down four years later off the coast of Honduras. John Smith now sails a fiberglass boat, something he'd vowed never to do. His whereabouts are unknown.

Billy Bones built his chandlery to support the wooden fleets involved in cargo shipping and fishing. He worried that losing this tradition would leave the planet feeling lonelier.

He single-handedly organized and maintained the boat regattas, donating a substantial amount of his own money and raising additional funds from other sources. He agreed with Linton Rigg that if they stopped the regattas, they would lose the fleet.

I told Bones about my wish to go fishing with one of the workboats.

He said, "Hope McLawrence of the *Imagine* is the guy you want to go with. He's the best fisherman in the fleet."

I took the bus to Windward, telling the driver I was searching for Hope McLawrence, and he took me right there.

I met Hope outside, cleaning the yard where he lived with his cousin in their seafront concrete home. I told Hope I was studying the working fleet, having developed one myself in Nicaragua. He invited me in for a beer, and we sat at the table overlooking the bay.

I asked how he'd started fishing. As a young boy, he used to take his family's homemade 14-foot sailing skiff to Tobago Cay for days at a time. While Tobago Cay now hosts many cruising sailors, it was the only boat there back then. He dried his catch in the sun and sailed his little boat to Grenada to sell his fish.

His mother worried about him being out for days, never knowing for sure if he'd come back. Finally, she convinced him to move to England to live with relatives and look for "real work." He lived in the UK for twenty-one years, finding a job in a brewery and then running a laundry. His love for fishing and the sea never left him.

After raising two sons, he returned to Carriacou with the money he'd earned and bought the locally built 37-foot deck sloop *Imagine*. He had sailed and fished ever since. He said you could make a living fishing, but it was hard work. Hope preferred to go out for days at a time—it was easier than coming in every day. I asked if I could crew with him in the morning. He agreed over a second bottle of beer.

The next morning at 6:30, I met Hope and his crew member, Gordon. Hope and Gordon were in their sixties but hardly missed a day's fishing.

We rowed the six-foot skiff a short distance to the *Imagine*, which was lazily at anchor. Hope and Gordon wasted no time setting sail and getting underway. The other boats were bustling with activity, each crew eager to be the first to leave. The competitive spirit was strong among the crews.

Outside the reef, Hope cast out his trolling lines to fish as we sailed fifteen miles to the fishing grounds off Saline Rock. It wasn't long before we pulled in a barracuda—first catch of the day.

After sailing for two and a half hours to find the right spot, we hove to and drift-fished with hand lines. Gordon went forward, I was amidships, and Hope fished over the stern, hauling in three butterfish at a time. Butterfish are bright red with blue spots and belong to the grouper family. They fetch $1.50 U.S. per pound from local buyers, while barracuda sells for $1.75.

As the day went on, our conversation ranged from boatbuilding to fishing, to John Smith and his loves won and lost. Hope worried he wouldn't have enough money to careen the *Imagine* for the repairs needed and to paint the bottom.

Hope said the boat builders on Bequia were the best. He told me the story of a 109-foot schooner built and crewed by Bequia boys that ran aground on the reef in Tobago Cay, ripping off part of the keel. They filled the hold with fifty-five-gallon drums, hauled the schooner off the reef, turned the ship upside down while at sea, and repaired the keel. They righted her, pumped her dry, and sailed away. It was a fantastic feat, but not surprising for those who build their boats on the beach among the mangroves.

By three-thirty in the afternoon, it was time to head in before dark. We had sixty pounds of fish on deck.

For the race home, we raised our headsail, and the other boats did the same. There were nine boats in the Windward fishing fleet: *Imagine, Margeta O, Pipe Dream, Chalib Sea, Glacier, Mary Stella, Rosalina, American Dream*, and *Run Away.*

As we sailed in, I reflected on a tough day's work fishing with hand lines and the challenge of surviving in what many see as paradise. When we arrived, we sold our catch and secured the boat. I thanked Hope and Gordon for a great day.

I understood why Captain Bully preferred motor over sail. How easy it would be to abandon sailing for power and let Carriacou's ongoing traditions become just another chapter in history books. Making it happen is a challenge. For Billy Bones, John Smith, Hope, Gordon, and others committed to Carriacou's sailing workboats, it is a deliberate choice to keep tradition alive.

Leaving Windward, I went past the graveyard with its many headstones. One name, Bernard Stewart, drew my attention. Next to his name was the carving of a schooner named *Gertrude B.* Above the carving was inscribed "Sailing on the Seas of Time."

In Carriacou, they sail on the seas of time.

GRENADA

After two years of building speculative houses in Virginia, I got a call from Kevin Sanderson at World Relief, informing me that Hurricane Ivan had struck the island of Grenada in the Caribbean. He had secured a significant amount of funding for reconstruction and asked me to oversee the project. Having visited the area a few years earlier, I was familiar with it. When I arrived in Grenada, I scarcely recognized the place. It looked as if a giant lawnmower had torn across the island. Most of the resorts along the beaches had been destroyed.

Two young men, Tony and Jason, stayed in one of the few hotels still standing. The guest house I had previously stayed in was destroyed. Tony, the country director for the project, had no idea how to restart things. Exhausted, he wanted to leave.

The first thing we did was set up an office. We found a duplex a hundred feet from Prickly Bay with a pool, which cheered them up as we settled in.

Tony had one month left on his contract. I assigned him to organize the office, which included setting up Internet service, updating finances, and opening a bank account.

Jason managed field operations. From central Canada, when he wasn't working on development projects, he took contracts planting trees for reforestation in the outback. I went out to see the projects he was working on here. The problem was that he didn't have much to start with because materials were hard to find.

I saw materials arriving on the island for rebuilding, but I needed to figure out how to access them. Materials were stored in a large building yard. I arranged a meeting with the owner to ask about accessing the materials. We needed an account, so we set one up.

That was one problem solved. Now we could go to work.

Prickly Bay was a popular spot for international sailors. I met the sailing crew at the Tiki Bar on the beach, where they gathered to swap sea stories. One man, a retired accountant, had sailed over from England. He and his wife lived on their boat. During our conversation, I mentioned our project to him, and he inquired about how he could assist us.

When he offered to donate his time, a light bulb went off in my head. We needed to establish an accounting system. I asked if he would be willing to work with us. He'd be happy to. When could he start? he asked,

I asked, how about tomorrow?

The next morning, he arrived early and reviewed our books. They were a mess. He organized them properly, introduced a voucher system, and we advertised for a bookkeeper to keep track of the records.

Several local women responded. We scheduled interviews with the applicants and chose Mariam, a mother of two young boys whose husband owned the local auto body shop. She adapted well to his system, and I worked with her until I left. She became my right hand.

Tony's contract ended, and he left as quickly as possible. I was glad to see him go—he had been a drag on the whole operation. Still, he was helpful because he introduced me to other international non-governmental organizations (NGOs). I was able to gather information from them and sometimes collaborate.

I learned from one of the NGOs that USAID was establishing an office in St. George to distribute grants for reconstruction. I arranged to meet with one of their distribution officers. They had $60 million available. The catch was that NGOs in the US could receive a one-time $25,000 grant, but for local Grenadian NGOs, there was no limit.

We began the grant process immediately. It was challenging because I needed information from the headquarters in Baltimore. I connected Mariam with our main office, and she promptly completed the application forms with the necessary details. We submitted everything to the USAID office in St. George, and they approved our application.

Once we understood the process, I asked Mariam if she wanted to start a Grenadian NGO to access more U.S. funding. She felt it would be too much for her, but she introduced me to Pastor Steve Worm, whom Jason had met while doing work for him.

I asked Pastor Steve if his church would start a Grenadian NGO. He was okay with it. Setting up a local NGO that met government requirements was complicated, but thanks to Steve Worm, the process got underway.

The primary requirement from USAID was that participants had to demonstrate land ownership. Much of the land had been passed down through families without deeds or official records. We needed to develop a method to establish ownership, so I assigned that task to Mariam.

We drafted affidavits to be signed by three residents in the parish, confirming that the families we are helping are the legal residents of the property. The local magistrate, along with a local priest or pastor, had to verify and sign the affidavit.

We submitted the affidavit to the USAID funding agency, and they accepted it.

Grenada was ideal for diving and snorkeling. As a dedicated snorkeler, I took advantage of it on weekends. I asked Jason if he wanted to go diving with me. He said he'd love to, but he didn't know how to swim. I told him I could teach him.

I bought him a set of swim fins, a mask, and a snorkel. At the pool in front of our office, I showed him how to put them on. Using the fins, he was swimming back and forth across the pool in no time. We added the mask and snorkel so he could submerge his face in the water and breathe through the snorkel.

The next step was taking him to Prickly Bay. We repeated the process in shallow water, then in deeper water over his head. It took an hour and a half, and he was snorkeling all around the bay. He loved it so much I could hardly get him out of the water.

Prickly Bay had a dive shop that offered lessons. When he came ashore, I suggested he should sign up for one of the classes. He walked over to the dive shop, dripping wet with fins and a snorkel in hand, and signed up. After finishing the course and getting his dive certificate, he went out every weekend for deep-water dives. I had a convert!

With the formalities complete, we began working earnestly. We hired Junior, a highly skilled and hardworking individual. I tasked him with procuring materials for each project and ensuring they were delivered to the site. To carry out the work, we hired local tradesmen supervised by Jason. Ultimately, we built or repaired 200 homes.

During the nine months I spent in Grenada, Juliet visited twice. It was always a pleasure to have her, even if only for a short stay. When she came, we stayed at La Sagesse, a beautiful old mansion with the same name.

It was there that Juliet told me about the discomfort in her hip. She started taking more potent pain medications to find some relief. I was worried, but I trusted the doctor's assessment that it was probably a sciatic problem. Over time, even the most potent drugs only dulled the pain.

I received a call from the head office in Baltimore. It was time to shut down because we had run out of money. Steve Worm and his group became a local NGO in Grenada. Handing everything over to him, I packed my things and headed home.

Nias Island

Before finishing the project in Grenada, the tsunami hit Indonesia. I was asked to take on a project on Nias Island. My role was supposed to be that of Country Director of Operations, but it didn't turn out that way.

Nias is a small island off the coast of Sumatra, Indonesia. It measures about 35 by 85 miles and has a population of around 300,000. They were struck by an 8.8 magnitude earthquake after the one that caused the tsunami. The north side of the island dropped nine meters, the south side rose eleven meters, and the entire island shifted twelve meters to the north.

In the middle, it cracked open like an egg. When it cracked open, entire villages were swallowed up and buried by the fissures. It was total devastation.

I boarded a plane at Newark Airport for a direct eighteen-hour flight to Singapore. I spent three days there obtaining my visa for Medan, the capital of Sumatra. World Relief rented an old bank building in Medan. It established its headquarters, primarily focusing on work in the Banda Aceh area on the island of Sumatra, where the tsunami had caused the most severe destruction.

Upon arriving in Medan, I was greeted by a staff member, taken to a guesthouse, and shown to my room. Medan's population was 2.1 million. Traffic in the city was terrible; Honda motorcycles filled every available space on the roads.

The central headquarters building downtown was bustling with activity and busy work. I was greeted there by Paul, the associate director, and we went to lunch at an open-air seafood restaurant. The prawns were fantastic and affordable.

After exchanging small talk and getting to know each other, I was informed that I would be working for Paul. That was completely different from what I was informed when I took the job. I could tell immediately we were going to face problems. I didn't say anything, planning to wait and see how things unfolded. Looking back, I should have stood my ground and told him I didn't need him.

Paul told me his Indonesian wife, two others, and I would fly out to Nias in two days. I spent those two days acclimating myself to the area and the organization's inner workings. Unimpressed with what I found, I observed a lot of busy work with little to no progress being made. What I saw in the first two days only got worse as time went on.

We flew to Nias early in the morning aboard a twin-engine propeller plane that seated thirty people. The aircraft was made in Indonesia, an older model but still comfortable. I later found out that most people were afraid to fly in it.

Flying over the channel into Nias was an awe-inspiring view: clear blue water dotted with tropical islands. Several volcanoes were visible from the windows. It resembled paradise.

I thought, this might not be so bad after all. That would soon change.

We arrived at a small airport outside the capital of Gunungsitoli. Paul and his wife had been there before, doing assessments, and knew their way around. Paul hired a van with a driver who was waiting to pick us up.

Taken to a small beachside hotel, I was amazed it had survived. House after house, building after building, were piles of rubble. The downtown area was completely flattened. The death toll was staggering. Backhoes and bulldozers cleared debris. There was a strong UN presence; white trucks and Toyota Land Cruisers with the black UN logo on their doors were everywhere.

We spent three days in Nias. Paul had a busy schedule planned for us. He contacted several local NGOs to explore partnership opportunities that would help him realize his vision for the island. His vision differed significantly from my original role. He wanted to start a children's health program, while I was hired for reconstruction. Paul wasn't interested in reconstruction. We ended up in trouble.

Down the coast, twenty miles away, Paul wanted to start one of his health programs to teach young children how to brush their teeth. The road was so bad that it took us hours to get there. The village was just a short walk from the beach. I told Paul we could have arrived in twenty minutes if we had a boat.

He responded, "No boats."

I asked him why.

He said no boats because he gets seasick.

One of the people with us was a healthcare worker. She came up with several songs that promoted good dental hygiene. I was not going to sing these songs to encourage children to keep their teeth clean, and I made that clear to Paul. I could no longer hide my feelings. From that point on, our relationship became strained, to say the least.

The group left to go back to Medan, and I decided to stay behind. I wanted to experience the place without Paul's distractions. They bought me a Honda 125 for transportation before they left. Gas was scarce on the island. Hundreds of Honda motorcycles lined up at the gas stations that still had fuel. It took hours to fill my two-gallon tank.

A large German man running a small German NGO told me he was staying at a Catholic convent operated by German nuns. The convent had rooms that the nuns allowed people to stay in if they were helping with the reconstruction.

I found the convent above the town and met with the head Sister. She gave me a room to stay in. I asked what they charged for a room, and she told me I could pay whatever I was willing to. The good part was that they served meals in a dining hall on the grounds. It was quite a find because it had an internet hookup. It became my headquarters for the rest of my time on Nias.

One of the sisters was running a makeshift orphanage for thirty-five children who had lost their parents in the earthquake. In my budget for room and board, I split the costs evenly between their accommodation and the sister caring for them. Because they were Catholic, Paul disapproved, but I did it anyway.

At a UN cluster meeting, I met a Japanese woman who was the head of the UN shelter delegation. She mentioned that she and her team needed a place to stay. I told her the convent rooms were available, and they moved in the next day.

The UN had an Australian engineering team called "Red R" contracted to design earthquake-resistant housing. These Australian guys were friendly and fun to hang out with. When they learned I was there to design a shelter, they included me in their group, and we created a shelter that became the standard for the island.

The best part about working with these Australians was receiving invites to their nighttime activities. Those fun times helped break up the monotony of the sixteen weeks I spent in Indonesia.

Working with our headquarters team in Medan became almost impossible. I couldn't commit to anything because the finance office was so disorganized that they refused to release funds. A lot of money was spent on headquarters infrastructure, but very little of it reached the field.

Returning to Medan for our progress meeting, the people working in Banda Aceh shared the same complaint. The situation was a disaster caused by poor leadership. Paul was determined to start a children's health program on Nias, and his decisions eventually took precedence over mine. Realizing I was in the wrong place, I established a headquarters building on the island and hired a young local lawyer to manage it, not knowing how much more I could handle working with Paul.

Surprisingly, one day I received a letter from Bill, Juliet's father. Bill had retired from the Daily Telegraph in London but still wrote a weekly column for the paper. He was interested in how the recovery efforts were progressing in Indonesia and wanted to include a piece about it in his column.

I gave him a rundown on the progress being made. He edited it and published it in next week's paper. I felt honored that he asked me because until then, I was considered four degrees lower than the family dog.

After sixteen weeks, I took a trip home. While there, I realized I wouldn't be returning under those conditions and decided to resign. Before I left, I felt I needed to inform the people in Baltimore about what was happening in Indonesia.

I called Kevin and poured out my heart. I blew the whistle on the entire operation. Kevin took my words seriously. He went to the CEO, a retired submarine commander, and shared my concerns.

I later discovered that the CEO had taken an emergency trip to Indonesia to assess the situation, confirming my report. Ultimately, the country director was reassigned, and Paul was dismissed immediately.

The irony was that Paul got a job with a different NGO whose task was to build shelter on Nias Island.

Military Training Exercises

World Relief was approached by the U.S. Army to participate in its annual Peacekeeping Operations (PKO) exercises in South America. The goal of these exercises was to coordinate with Latin American countries in computer-simulated disasters while collaborating with NGOs.

World Relief didn't want to participate, but Kevin thought that, given my military background, I might be interested in going. Of course, I wanted to go!

The first exercise was held in Quito, Ecuador. The Army flew me to a hotel large enough to accommodate delegations from twenty-one Latin American countries.

I was taken to the NGO's operational headquarters and shown my cubicle, complete with a computer and a copy of the scenario. They had invited several NGOs, but I was the only one who showed up, so I had the cubicle to myself.

The scenario involved a fictional country affected by a natural disaster during a military conflict. The military was tasked with maintaining stability to support relief efforts led by the United Nations and major NGOs.

The exercise was well-scripted. I didn't know what to do, and nobody provided instructions. Sitting in my cubicle, watching the scenario unfold on the computer, I noticed gaps on the NGO side that needed to be addressed. On my own initiative, I began introducing NGO problems into the scenario that the military side had to handle, such as food delivery robberies, materials held for ransom, road washouts, and abandoned orphanages in need of urgent care and rescue.

The planners were unaware of the origins of these issues; they weren't part of the original plan. When they learned I was responsible, they came to my cubicle for a visit. I thought I was in trouble when they barged in, but I realized they were actually impressed with what I was doing and wanted me to keep going.

When the first PKO was finished, the planners asked me to join the planning team for future exercises. I saw it as my patriotic duty.

For the next four years, these exercises were the highlight of my year. I could hardly wait for each one. The Army treated me well and kept me updated. After Quito, I traveled with them to Nicaragua, Uruguay, Chile, and Brazil.

After Brazil, the U.S. economy suffered a crash. The military faced severe financial cutbacks and had to eliminate the PKO exercises. I was disappointed.

Haiti Mission

I was sent to develop shelter recovery efforts in Haiti after the devastating earthquake struck the island. Excited to be involved, I told Kevin I'd prefer to go as an independent consultant. My experience influenced my decision in Indonesia; I didn't want to go through that again. Kevin agreed, and I signed a contract as a shelter consultant. I worked independently and managed the budget for the shelter program.

The Haiti disaster was a UN operation I was familiar with. The leadership team of World Relief was dedicated to the mission but lacked experience in disaster relief and wasn't sure where to begin. They were happy to let me take charge of the shelter aspect.

There is disappointing news for those hoping for a positive outlook on Haiti's future. I met remarkable and dedicated people, but the leadership was riddled with corruption. For instance, World Relief shipped three Land Cruisers for transportation, yet their government refused to release them from customs because they wanted us to lease vehicles or buy them from local vendors at inflated prices.

Crime was widespread. There were places you avoided, zones controlled by mafia-like groups. Shots echoed through the night, roads were dangerous, filth was everywhere, and voodoo areas felt creepy, but surprisingly, life went on.

The house we used was a large, old mansion painted pink, called The White House. I asked why a pink house was named the White House. I was told it used to be the hub for white powder cocaine trafficking.

Robison, who was from Gonave Island, was a shining light. His honesty was unwavering, which made sense once you understood Gonave's culture.

Parishes with strict disciplinary rules manage Gonave. If you break a rule, it's difficult to escape on an island. Once caught, you face a high cost, sometimes painfully, and are then banned from the island. Robison was raised under those rules, and I found him invaluable.

The first step was to contact the UN shelter manager and find a space where we could work without interfering with other NGOs doing the same work. I hired two local people to help me and visited the designated sites, reaching out to those in need of shelter.

Haiti faced the same land tenure problem as Grenada; there was no record showing that these people owned the property. Having already addressed this issue in Grenada, we used the same process. All parties, including the UN, approved it.

A group was already producing prefab units similar to those used in the Nicaraguan housing project. Instead of reinventing the wheel, we bought 125 prefabricated units. The price included on-site delivery.

Adding to the Haitian crisis, a cholera epidemic broke out across the island while I was there. It was caused by Pakistani UN Peacekeepers, an embarrassment for the UN delegation, which resulted in the death of many Haitians. I worked briefly with a medical NGO to deliver essential medicine to affected areas. Some roads were so bad that supplies had to be flown in by helicopter.

This project went smoothly. In three months, we finished our task, and I was back home.

The Long Goodbye

Juliet's Sickness and Passing

Back home, I resumed building houses for friends and created a few that we kept, which eventually led to starting a rental business. Juliet was registered with the Health Department and her church. She had found a niche for herself and was happy where she was.

She learned about medical mission teams heading to the Dominican Republic to work in small mountain villages. Fluent in Spanish, she applied and was accepted to join the team. Every year, she spent her vacation there.

Her hip problem persisted and worsened. We kept visiting different doctors, trying to figure out what was wrong. The diagnosis consistently pointed to a possible sciatic nerve issue that could be fixed with physical therapy.

The pain became so intense that she finally had an MRI to determine the exact cause. The MRI revealed her back was healthy, but they couldn't pinpoint the reason. The only option was more therapy.

She pushed through and kept working, but she came home crying from the pain. I felt so helpless and worried sick.

Finally, she came home, said she couldn't go back to work, and went to bed. She looked extremely pale, had lost weight, and was unable to work. I knew she was dying.

I went to see our doctor and told him I thought Juliet was dying and that something needed to be done. He said he'd come by after work to check her out. When he arrived, he was shocked by her condition and told me to take her to his office the next morning.

I bundled her up and took her in. After examining her, he decided to admit her to the local hospital that same day.

I took her to the hospital and helped her get admitted. They put her in a room and administered strong pain medication. That same day, they performed an MRI to pinpoint precisely where the pain was coming from. The doctor informed us that they had found a mass. They didn't know what it was and planned to do a biopsy. She needed to go to another hospital for the procedure, and I was supposed to take her in the morning.

The doctor at the second hospital had already reviewed the MRI from the first hospital by the time we arrived. He had identified the issue. No one told us anything, but they said she needed to go to VCU Hospital in Richmond for further tests. They took her there by ambulance. I went home to gather her personal items, planning to meet her there as soon as possible.

When I arrived, they were conducting several tests. I waited in her room until she returned. When they wheeled her in, she looked better thanks to the medications they had given her. She was tired, but we talked, avoiding the main issue.

A nurse came in to inform us that a doctor would be visiting to consult with us. I was hungry and went down to the cafeteria to get a sandwich.

When I returned, the doctor was in the room waiting. Then he delivered the news: Juliet had a stage four pleomorphic sarcoma. There was nothing they could do; it was a terminal condition. He gave her two months to live. My greatest fear had come true.

Uncertain of what to do and at the mercy of the medical staff, they moved her to another room and gave her drugs through different tubes. I called her sisters to tell them about the situation. Overcome with emotion, I started crying as I described her condition.

One of her sisters lived in England, and the other was in Australia. They each booked the next available flight to arrive here within three days.

The hospital staff brought in a large recliner for me. They placed it beside Juliet's bed, and I stayed with her day and night. She was declining quickly. Juliet told me she didn't want any more tubes or drugs; she wanted to go home and sleep in her own bed. I agreed and told the staff our wishes. They asked several times to make sure they understood what we meant. Honoring our request meant we would need to stay a couple of days in palliative care to determine what pain medicine she needed to stay comfortable.

The next day, her sister arrived from England. I picked her up from the airport and brought her to our house to relax and recover from her trip. First thing in the morning, we went to the hospital. She stayed with Juliet while I went back home to arrange for hospice to bring a hospital bed into our bedroom.

The hospice staff was incredible; they truly knew their jobs. They organized everything to ensure Juliet was well cared for. Juliet's other sister, Jill, arrived and took a taxi directly to the hospital. The three sisters spent the night together.

Juliet arrived home the next day via ambulance. I went to the hospital and picked up her sisters. I had prepared the house for their arrival, and the neighbors began bringing over lots of food, showing concern and helpfulness.

After Juliet arrived and we got her into bed, the hospice nurses explained how to give the pain medication. All we could do now was wait for the end.

Watching someone you love die is horrible. Her sisters decided to care for Juliet until she passed away, not wanting anyone else to get involved. That plan lasted until the third night, when they finally broke down, completely exhausted.

At two in the morning, Jill yelled, "I DIDN'T KNOW IT WOULD BE LIKE THIS!"

I called one of the nurses Juliet worked with and apologized for calling so early. She said she didn't mind, she was expecting it, and came right over. Nurses from Juliet's workplace organized themselves into shifts, coming day and night. They made sure she was as comfortable as possible. The food kept coming.

Adding to the drama, I built a house for Juliet using money from her inheritance. Although the will stated it was mine because all I had would belong to her, her sisters gathered and argued that it should be returned to the family. I was caught off guard by this revelation, as I had built it. How do you argue with someone on her deathbed?

It became a point of contention. I had my investment in the property and didn't want it to go to the sisters. I told them that if they gave me my share of the investment, they could have the house. It became very awkward when they sought legal advice on how to circumvent me. They didn't have a leg to stand on—the will was clear.

Three weeks after Juliet came home from the hospital, she died peacefully, surrounded by her sisters and closest friends. She was gone.

Her sisters stayed until the memorial service the following week. I was scheduled to speak, and it wouldn't be easy. On the day of the service, the church was filled with people who loved and admired Juliet. I talked about our life together, including our travels around the world and our various projects. Jon and Sharon came from California.

Kevin also attended, and after the service, the church served an excellent meal.

Her sisters and I packed up family treasures and sent them to England and Australia, including the family silverware. They left me without any knives, forks, or spoons. Lucy, Juliet's younger sister, requested that Juliet's ashes be sent back to England and scattered at Goodenstone Park, the family estate. I agreed. One of Juliet's friends took her sisters to the airport after blunted goodbyes.

The house was empty except for my memories and me.

Your Have a Life to Live - Go Live it

Reflection

After the initial honeymoon phase, I believe Juliet wondered why she had ever married. Our cultures were so different that we constantly stepped on each other's toes. Because of her upbringing, she had built a protective barrier around her life and emotions that I kept crossing. I wasn't a sensitive guy. I thought we shared a common vision for our lives, but looking back, she was always trying to catch up. She never considered divorce; her honor in taking the marriage vows wouldn't allow it. She did say that if I wanted out, she would grant it. I didn't want to break up. I loved her.

When we moved to Virginia, we established a routine: she lived her life, I lived mine. Then came cancer. You don't do well if you don't feel well. She had it for years, all the while being told it was something else. When not working, she spent most of her time with a select group from her church during long prayer vigils. She was happiest when I was away on my trips, but she tolerated me while I was home. I built her a house and gave her space, accepting the fleeting moments when we connected.

One day, as I was reflecting on our life together, I heard a voice say, "You have a life to live. Go live it."

Epilogue

I was told I needed to write this story, which took me two and a half years. Recently, I learned that 22 combat veterans take their own lives every day.

The number shocked me.

I immediately related to the symptoms because I experienced the same struggle when I returned from Vietnam, as I share in this book. From these pages, we are now working on creating a documentary to reach out to struggling veterans, so they know they are not alone. Others have gone before them, who understand their fight, and through healing, have reclaimed their lives.

I realized I had to get involved in something bigger than myself, and that experience ultimately led to a more fulfilling life. This is not the end of the story but just the beginning, as we all work together to save lives and offer hope and purpose.

For the latest update on the documentary, please check out www.mysoultokeepllc.com

Acknowledgements

So many people have come and gone in my life. I don't know where to begin.

I guess I should start with my mom. I remember her saying, "I try, I try. The lord knows I try. If you only knew how much I love you." She did try, and she did love me. I was more than happy to support her in her time when she needed what I needed as a young child.

There are my drill instructors and the Marines I fought with in Vietnam. War is so horrible; it takes the love of my fellow Marines to get through it. There are only a handful of us left, but we still stay in touch. And when we are together, it's like we never left. What an honor to be known by such men. Semper Fi, Brothers.

There are those who helped me get through my crisis. Too many to name, but I want to thank you all. A special shout-out to Rob Bodie and Sharon Omey—they worked together to secure my teaching job, which truly changed my life. Bob Trolese and Alfred Kultsmitt were genuine friends. The housing project revealed our true character. What a team. Kevin Sanderson stands out. He believed in me as Latin American Director for World Relief. Through him, I traveled the world and experienced a life I never would have imagined.

My friends here in Virginia took us in, and you couldn't 2nd better neighbors. Mead Usry was one. He told me to write. It was a struggle at first, but now it's therapy.

Wayne and Caroljn from Amsterdam. Somehow, they always show up wherever I might be on the planet.

I'm forgetting so many more, but I can't leave out Jeanne Johansen, publisher at High Tide Publications. She never lets me quit until I get it right.

Thank you all. You are forever loved.

Bob

About the Author

Bob Means joined the Marines at seventeen and was deployed to Vietnam, where he faced intense combat and was wounded. After struggling with PTSD and a nervous breakdown, he found purpose in disaster relief work.

He built orphanages and maternity clinics in Vietnam and Guatemala. After his wife's passing, he wrote his memoir, *Courage*, which we're seeking partners to make into a documentary film, to bring awareness to the epidemic of veterans suffering from PTSD and suicide.

Bob now resides on his private golf course in Urbanna, Virginia.

Made in the USA
Monee, IL
03 November 2026

67384100R00157